Willa Cather

The Works of Willa Cather

ぞ

WILLA
CATHER

Barbara Bonham

CHILTON BOOK COMPANY
Philadelphia / New York / London

For Leanne, Mark and Patty, who share a pioneer heritage

one

Life in the lush Shenandoah Valley of Virginia and life on the raw Nebraska prairie in the 1870's could not have been more different if an ocean had lain between them. Life in Virginia had a smoothness and a sense of permanency that were to make the move to the rough frontier a bone-rattling shock to a child as sensitive and impressionable as Willa Sibert Cather. It was to color her life and her writing until the day she died.

Willa Cather was born on December 7, 1873, in her Grandmother Boak's house in the village of Back Creek, Virginia. Soon after she was born, her parents and her grandmother moved to Willowshade farm a few miles away. The three-story brick house at Willowshade had been built by Grandfather Cather on the banks of a quiet stream. William Cather had so placed the house that the stream wound its way through the front yard among the leafy willows that gave the farm its name.

Willa Cather found life at Willowshade full and fascinating—serene but never dull. A large number of people, both black and white, were hired to work about the farm. There were the fields to be tended and a never-ending round of tasks to be done around the house—sewing, spinning, quilting, churning, preserving, candlemaking, butchering and curing.

Occasionally tin peddlers or broom-makers stopped by and were lodged overnight in the wing at the back of the house. These visitors held a special attraction for Willa Cather and she once opened her bank to give Uncle Billy Parks, a broom-maker, all the money in it as a token of her esteem.

She was a pretty child with an abundance of long, reddish-brown hair, but her clear blue eyes were her most extraordinary feature. They missed nothing, seeming to see more and deeper than did ordinary eyes.

She was an unusually imaginative child and liked nothing better than to have stories told or read to her. It was her Grandmother Boak she coaxed most often into doing this. There were few, if any, books written especially for children in those days, so her grandmother read to her from the Bible and *The Pilgrim's Progress*. She absorbed these two books as she absorbed her Southern accent; she lost the accent, but the books remained forever a part of her. Their influence was to be present in everything she wrote, from dramatic criticism to her novels.

Another book from which Grandmother Boak read to her was Peter Parley's *Universal History*. Although it must have been largely incomprehensible to so young a mind as Willa's, she wrung some impressions from it. Her parents found that they could keep her quiet for long periods by building a chariot for her from two chairs, one atop the other. She would drive this chariot in complete silence while an imaginary slave ran beside her, repeating at intervals, *"Cato, thou art but man!"*

Willa never attended school in Virginia, yet by the time the family left for Nebraska, she was probably more familiar with Shakespeare and English history than most children of nine years who attended school regularly— thanks to her Grandmother Boak, who not only read to her but taught her to read. Reading, once learned, became a necessity; a life without books and reading would have been intolerable for her.

She proceeded to learn the heroic literature of Homer, Vergil, and the Norsemen. The seas those ancients sailed, the islands they touched, became as real to her as the villages and hills of Virginia. Then there was the enchantment of *The Arabian Nights,* Grimm's *Fairy Tales,* and Roman and Greek mythology. As a result of this reading, her mind became as richly furnished as an Arabian Nights' palace.

Before Willa learned how to read for herself, she discovered another source of stories. There was a group of women—most of them old—who would come down into the valley from Timber Ridge and make quilts for various families. When they came to Willowshade, Willa would crawl under the quilting frames and sit there listening to those women relate in their soft Southern voices the dramatic events that had become legends of the countryside.

A few of the stories concerned her own family, for Grandfather Cather had been a Northern sympathizer during the Civil War, a fact that was very painful to his father, brothers, and sisters. Once when the Confederates were planning to raid the farms of Northern sympathizers, a neighbor warned William Cather, saying, "Bring your stock over to my barn and they'll be safe." William Cather accepted the offer and later, when Union forces were planning to raid the farms of Confederates, he returned the favor.

The Boaks, too, were individualists, so it is not surprising that Willa grew up to be fearless in matters of thought and social convention. She was never afraid to be different if her natural inclinations led her that way—and they usually did.

She inherited her strong will from her mother. Mary Virginia Boak was a handsome woman, the kind who never stepped out of her bedroom without being perfectly groomed. She allowed no one to see her until her long, dark hair had been pinned up. It was she who dominated the family. Although she ruled her children with a firm hand—even using a rawhide whip when it was necessary to punish them—she had their complete and unswerving devotion. Despite her sternness, she had unusual sympathy for and understanding of her children's individuality. So long as they observed the rules of the household, she gave them complete freedom to carry out all the schemes and projects they dreamed up.

There were seven Cather children: Willa, Roscoe, Douglass, and Jessica were born in Virginia; James, John, and Elsie, in Nebraska. Willa, the oldest, was named for her grandfathers, both of whom were named William. Although her parents named her Wilella and even recorded it so in the family Bible, they changed her name almost immediately to Willa, and Willa or "Willie" she remained. When she grew older, she cut the name Wilella from the family Bible and substituted the name Willa. She also altered her birth date so that she would appear two years younger than she actually was. Throughout her life Willa Cather fought the passage of time and the changes it brought.

Charles Cather, Willa's father, was a gentle man with a cheerful disposition. Before his marriage he had read law in a law office in Washington, D.C. He was tall and fair-haired with gracious, courtly manners. Willa adored her father and was proud of the fact that her own fine skin and dark blue eyes were like his. He called her "Daughter" and even after she became famous, he could not believe she had grown up.

Willa Cather was an exceptional individual even as a child. One day when she was five years old, a son of one of the servants came into the room where she was playing. A half-witted boy, he told Willa he meant to cut off her hand with the knife he was carrying.

The room in which Willa was playing was upstairs and there was no one close enough to rescue her. She was badly frightened but realized that she must not show it. Coaxing the boy to a window, she showed him a tall tree that grew close by, its branches almost touching the house. She persuaded him that it would be fun to climb out on one of the branches and make his way to the ground. The boy forgot what he had threatened and climbed down the tree.

There was another simpleminded person at Willow-shade, but this one was not dangerous in the least. Margie Anderson was the daughter of one of the women whose stories Willa loved to listen to as she sat beneath the quilting frames. Margie served the Cather family as nursemaid and houseworker with perfect devotion. With Margie as a companion, Willa used to roam the woods and fields. Sometimes they went as far as Timber Ridge to visit Margie's mother and hear her stories. Willa seems to have understood what it meant to be as defenseless as Margie was. She loved the simple girl and felt a deep protectiveness toward her. When the Charles Cathers moved to Nebraska, Margie went with them and lived in their house until her death many years later.

George Cather, the brother of Willa's father, had taken his bride to Webster County, Nebraska, to homestead in 1873, the year Willa was born. His father joined him in 1877, buying a ranch in Webster County and leaving Willowshade in the hands of his other son, Charles. Since the land was poor, the chief industry at Willowshade was sheep raising. At night Charles Cather would carry his daughter on his shoulder as he went to drive the sheep into the fold. So vivid was this memory that it inspired Willa Cather years later to write a poem called "The Swedish Mother."

There was an enormous four-story barn at Willowshade containing a mill that ground feed for the sheep. One day a fire, started by spontaneous combustion, burned this barn to the ground. William Cather decided not to rebuild the barn but to sell Willowshade instead. Charles Cather, who had been considering moving to Nebraska ever since his brother and father had gone there, made preparations to join them.

There appears to have been no excitement on Willa's part about the move, only regret at leaving familiar and beloved things. One of the beloved things was her favorite sheep dog, Vic. Her father had made little leather shoes to protect Vic's feet from sharp stones. Vic used to come up to Willa or her father and beg for those shoes before they started out after the sheep.

When the Charles Cather family said good-bye to Willowshade for the last time, Vic was left behind, chained up at a neighbor's house. Just as the family was boarding the train, Vic came running across the fields, dragging her broken chain. But it had been a futile escape. Vic had to be left behind, along with everything else in her life in Virginia that Willa loved passionately.

It is not at all surprising that she and the Nebraska prairie began their relationship as enemies.

two

The Charles Cather family arrived in Red Cloud, Nebraska, in April, 1883. The town was twelve years old and still had a raw, new look. Its main street, bordered by a broken line of wooden buildings, ran from the depot north for about a mile. Back of the buildings, and scattered haphazardly about the prairie, were a number of houses. Except for one thing—the trees—the whole town appeared as if it had been built to be used only a few years and then abandoned. Most of the trees had been dug up from the banks of the Republican River two miles south of town and planted around the houses. They were still small, those cottonwoods and box elders, but they proclaimed that this town was growing roots, too, and that it meant to last.

Still the town was bleak and ugly; the sight of it must have been painful to the eyes of a sensitive child. The towns in Virginia had had a century or two to become beautiful and gracious, full of huge trees, green lawns, and large houses surrounded by flowers and shrubs. Each house had an air of permanency, of belonging. Removing even one of them would have left as noticeable a gap as if one had lost a front tooth. In Red Cloud a house might have been blown away by the prairie wind and the loss would never have been apparent to a stranger.

It was when the family began the sixteen-mile trip by wagon to Catherton, north of Red Cloud, where the homesteads of her grandfather and uncle were located, that Willa must have felt she had stepped off the edge of the world. The Nebraska landscape was eerie in its emptiness. Virginia had been filled with mountains and trees, fields and houses, human beings. Here there was nothing but land stretching from horizon to horizon. It moved as the sea moves, covered with waving prairie grass reaching to a man's waist, dry and copper-red, hiding the new green growth that was beginning to emerge from the ground.

It was mournful and frightening and nine-year-old Willa hated it on sight. In an interview a number of years later, she recalled her first reaction to the Nebraska prairie:

"I shall never forget my introduction to it. We drove out from Red Cloud to my grandfather's homestead one day in April. I was sitting on the hay in the bottom of a Studebaker wagon, holding on to the side of the wagon box to steady myself—the roads were mostly faint trails over the bunch grass in those days. The land was open range and there was almost no fencing. As we drove further out into the country, I felt a good deal as if we had come to the end of everything—it was a kind of erasure of personality.

"I would not know how much a child's life is bound up in the woods and hills and meadows around it, if I had not been jerked away from all these and thrown out into a country as bare as a piece of sheet iron. I had heard my father say you had to show grit in a new country, and I would have got on pretty well during that ride if it had not been for the larks. Every now and then one flew up and sang a few splendid notes and dropped down into the grass again. That reminded me of something—I don't know what, but my one purpose in life just then was not to cry, and every time they did it, I thought I should go under."

Her first glimpse of her grandparents' house brought no comfort either. Rising starkly out of the prairie grass, it seemed only to emphasize the vast emptiness of the land. Huddled around it were a few outbuildings and a windmill. Once inside, however, enveloped in love and the familiar sounds of her grandparents' voices, she was able to forget the strange country that lay outside. How good it was to see Grandfather and Grandmother Cather again! Grandmother Boak had accompanied Willa's parents to Nebraska so the whole family would be reunited. As long as it existed, Willa Cather's family was to be a source of comfort and happiness. Nevertheless her homesickness for Virginia those first two weeks was so great that she could scarcely eat.

Shortly after Willa's arrival, Grandfather Cather returned to Virginia, probably to attend to matters of business, and Grandmother Cather moved in with her son George and his wife, Frances. That left the house to the Charles Cather family.

Her mother was ill much of that first year and Willa was allowed to do much as she pleased. For one thing, she chose to explore the thinly settled country on horseback. It was a cosmopolitan community: Bohemians,

Scandinavians, Germans, Frenchmen, as well as Americans from New England and some with Southern backgrounds like her own. The Nebraska Department of Immigration had advertised its cheap, rich land in countries all over Europe. It wanted people to settle the prairie and harvest its wealth so the state might grow and prosper. The opportunity to own land, a privilege only of the rich in Europe, brought many immigrants to Nebraska. Others, particularly the Bohemians, came to America because they did not approve of the government in their own country.

Someone who knew Willa Cather in those early years described her as "a young curiosity shop." It was this curiosity that took her into the sod houses of the immigrants, in which the native American pioneers seldom bothered to set foot. Twenty-five years later she expressed the impatience she still felt at the lack of curiosity demonstrated by her family and the other American settlers. They were kind enough to the immigrants, lending a hand to help any neighbor who was sick or in trouble, but that was as far as their involvement went. To Willa, however, those foreign-born pioneers opened a whole new world. Observing and associating with them taught her much about the nature of man and of this prairie country in which the Americans, as well as the Europeans, were aliens for a time.

About her visits to those sod houses and dugouts she later wrote:

"I have never found any intellectual excitement more intense than I used to feel when I spent a morning with one of these pioneer women at her baking or buttermaking. I used to ride home in the most unreasonable state of excitement; I always felt as if they had told me so much more than they said—as if I had got inside another person's skin."

The Bohemians in particular drew Willa. Many of them were refined, cultivated people, but she found just as much inspiration in the simpler type. From the first such group she drew her portrait of Papa Shimerda in her novel *My Ántonia*. The main character in her short story "Neighbor Rosicky" was developed from the latter group. Later she was to say that Rosicky's love of the land, combined with the satisfaction of hard work, a rugged spirit, and the refusal to admit defeat, was the very stuff of which Nebraska was made.

Willa Cather was not seeing those people as characters to be used in her writing, however. She had no thought then of becoming a writer. They interested her simply because they were different. The various cultures and customs she found in those pioneer homes fed her hungry intellectual curiosity and perhaps helped her accept the bleak prairie that had become her home. She came to feel, too, the excitement of the struggle that was being waged to tame that raw land, forcing it to submit to man's hand for the first time.

She was well aware that it was a grim struggle, that the land was not giving up easily. It opened its whole bag of tricks in its attempts to discourage the settlers. There were droughts that withered the crops, blizzards that smothered livestock, hailstorms that chopped the growing plants to shreds, and clouds of grasshoppers that ate crops and gardens down to the roots. The result was a battle that tried the souls of men. Some of them, physically and emotionally unfit for the hard struggle, broke. Others fought the land and it was their determination and their unwavering belief that they could overcome that inspired Willa. She was never to lose her admiration for the vigor and energy and endurance of those people.

Willa Cather's first playmate on the prairie was Leedy Lambrecht, the daughter of German immigrants. The two girls played in the attic of the Cather home, dressing in grown-up clothes, pretending to be clowns, or they went snake-hunting with Leedy's brother, Henry, who peeled sugarcane for them to eat.

Willa had considered the prairie ugly and frightening at first, but she had discovered it had its own peculiar kind of beauty that was to grip her and never let go. The ravines—or "draws" as they are called on the prairie— were brilliant with color from April until the first autumn frost. Early in the spring the plum thickets would burst into bloom. What had been the day before a mass of dead-looking twigs would be covered with white blossoms that made the air heavy with their sweetness. Later the sunflowers would bloom, the lushness of their color so eye-filling that one might almost miss the smaller and more modest snow-on-the-mountain and the purple iron-weed. In the fall the fuzzy spikes of the goldenrod appeared and finally, in one last glorious blaze of color before the countryside turned tan and gray, the draws would fill with red sumac. Willa had always loved flowers and she was delighted to find that the prairie she had at first thought so empty and ugly was full of flowering plants. She even came to love the coppery grass that covered the land in the same way an animal is covered with fur. She once described the prairie as appearing to have had red wine spilled on it.

After she became a woman, Willa looked back on that first summer on the prairie and wrote, "The country and I had it out together and by the end of the first autumn, that shaggy grass country had gripped me with a passion I have never been able to shake. It has been the happiness and the curse of my life."

❧

three

Willa's family lived on the Nebraska homestead for about a year-and-a-half and then Charles Cather, who was not cut out to be a farmer, moved his family into Red Cloud. There he went into business, selling insurance, making loans, and writing abstracts for which his training in law had prepared him.

The house into which the Cathers moved was a long, narrow frame house painted white. It stood only a block off Red Cloud's main street and its one and a half stories did not offer enough space for the large family. Willa did not like the place at first and she was always to resent the crowding. She found the house ugly and complained that the lumberman who built it had used leftovers and odd pieces. The gracious houses of Virginia, with their spacious rooms and large fireplaces, were too fresh in her memory.

Despite the fact that the house was too small, Charles Cather decided to remain in it and pay rent rather than build his own. He said it was better business for him to continue loaning his money out than to put it into a new house.

The house did contain one redeeming feature: Willa and her brothers, Roscoe and Douglas, were given the attic as a bedroom and playroom. That attic, so roughly finished that snow filtered through the roof and collected on blankets on winter nights, became a place of enchantment for Willa. There she could escape the crowded downstairs, dream her dreams, and read her favorite books. In her eyes it was no common bedroom; it was a feudal hall like those she read about in the sagas of the Norsemen.

When she grew older, one end of the attic was partitioned off for her. The small room was papered with a large rose pattern and came to be called "The Rose Bower." None of the other children were allowed in there and Willa treasured the quiet, private moments she was able to spend in that room. Later when she left for college, the room was closed and kept unchanged for her use when she came home.

Privacy was always necessary to Willa. One summer she put a canvas roof and sides on the upper front porch of the Cather house. It was an eyesore to which her parents objected strongly, but she refused to tear it down. She enjoyed sitting on that porch, but she did not want anyone gazing at her.

Red Cloud had grown and become firmly rooted in the prairie in the year-and-a-half since Willa's family had arrived in Nebraska. The population was now twenty-five hundred and the people envisioned even more growth and a great future for their community. In this the town was no different from the others that thrust up out of the prairie sod like mushrooms. As a matter of fact, it was quite an ordinary town, but there, in an environment seemingly so lacking in imaginative material, Willa found her richest source of experience. She was to return to it again and again in her novels—*My Ántonia, The Song of the Lark, A Lost Lady, One of Ours, Lucy Gayheart*—and in her short stories, just as she herself returned to it each summer so long as her parents were alive.

Later she did not think it strange that she found so much to write about in that prairie community. She declared that every place is a storehouse of literary material. "If a true artist were born in a pigpen and raised in a sty, he would still find plenty of inspiration for his work," she said. "The only need is the eye to see."

Red Cloud was extraordinary in one way, however: It contained a surprising number of brilliant and artistic people. They drew Willa like a magnet and she formed close and personal relationships with most of them. She met three of them when she began to attend school in Red Cloud and they were to affect her life profoundly. They were Mrs. Eva J. Case and Mr. and Mrs. A. K. Goudy. Mrs. Case taught literature and foreign languages. Mr. Goudy was superintendent of the school, and his wife was principal. All were unusually fine teachers and the first persons Willa had ever known with any intellectual background, any interest in ideas and the culture of the past. She always credited them with teaching her to think, to find her way in the world of imaginative thought. She felt that she owed to them the early ideals of scholarship and art that gave direction to her own life and work.

Mrs. Case was a remarkable woman with rare insight. She recognized Willa's exceptional nature and realized that it could be stifled in this small prairie town. She encouraged Willa to feed her mind with great books that would stimulate growth. Her friendship and understanding were a comfort in a community that was too often intolerant of anyone who was different.

Both the Goudys became attached to this unusual pupil. They found she had an amazing familiarity with classical English literature but could not spell correctly. She had a genuine love for Latin, yet she was ignorant of the ordinary things most other grade-school children knew. As a woman she once laughingly remarked that she had a degree from the University of Nebraska but still could not say her multiplication tables.

Her personality drew them too. It was so striking in its originality, its daring, and its vital force that no one could remain indifferent to Willa. She aroused either strong liking or intense antagonism—the Goudys liked her. Willa was delighted when Mr. Goudy became State Superintendent of Public Instruction and moved to Lincoln the same year she entered the University of Nebraska there. Mrs. Goudy was made Deputy State Superintendent. Willa saw them often, and the friendship was to last as long as the Goudys lived.

Several other gifted individuals in Red Cloud helped widen Willa's horizons. One of these was William Ducker, an Englishman of about sixty who had come to Red Cloud to work in his brother's store. A classical scholar, he was regarded as a failure and a dreamer by the hustling businessmen of Red Cloud, but Willa could not accept this estimate of him. She could regard as a failure no man who possessed his knowledge of the Latin and Greek classics. With Mr. Ducker she read Vergil, Ovid, Homer's *Iliad*, and some of the odes of Anacreon. They also discussed mind-stretching subjects like Christianity, evolution, good and evil. Willa was thirteen or fourteen when she began to read the classics with Mr. Ducker and she continued to read with him during her summer vacations from the university.

Peorianna Sill, who was named for the town in Illinois where she was born, stood out in the small prairie town of Red Cloud like a peacock in a flock of turtledoves. She and her husband, Calvin, had come to Nebraska to start a sheep ranch. When the venture failed, they moved into town. Mr. Sill made farm loans and Peorianna conducted classes in painting and in music. Some years earlier, while living in Europe, she had shown such promise as a musician that she had been accepted as a pupil by the composer Anton Rubinstein. She had also studied art for fifteen years and become so skillful that her copies of old masters could scarcely be told from the originals. Her glamour was enhanced by the story that the Queen of Italy, impressed with her talent, had allowed her to paint the Bay of Naples from the royal boudoir window.

The famous American writer Washington Irving, to whom Peorianna was related on her mother's side, had given her as a wedding gift a pair of teardrop earrings reportedly made with diamonds formerly belonging to Queen Isabella II of Spain, where Irving had served for a time as United States Ambassador. Wearing a gold velvet gown and her diamond earrings, while she conducted cantatas and musical programs, Mrs. Sill must have presented a vivid picture to a young girl like Willa, starved for beauty and culture.

Next door to the Cather house lived the Charles Wieners. Mr. Wiener was one of the merchants in Red Cloud, his wife a brilliant woman of French birth. The Wieners spoke French and German in their home and had collected a library unusual for its size and quality. Once acquainted with Willa, the Wieners became aware of her extraordinary mind and gave her the run of their house. They literally opened the door of a new world for her. On summer afternoons when her own attic room was stifling, she would go to their house and lie on the floor, reading their books and gazing at their paintings. Mrs. Wiener discussed French novels with Willa and began reading them to her, translating as she went along. Eventually Willa began to read French and to wish she could read German. She pored over books about Germany, France, and the rest of Europe. Mrs. Wiener lent her encouragement and urged her to study hard.

Another source of information about European life and culture was Professor Shindelmeisser, a German who made his living by giving music lessons. Music was to be important to Willa Cather as a source of joy and inspiration, but she was not interested in learning to play an instrument or to sing. When Professor Shindelmeisser came to give her a piano lesson, she interrupted the lesson constantly to ask him about Germany, about its cities, its customs, its language, its music. No argument he used could persuade her to practice or pay attention to the lesson.

Exasperated, he would go to his next pupil, sink exhaustedly into a chair and exclaim, "Vat vill I do vith that Villie Catter? Her folks vant her to have some music but all she vants to do is ask qvestions. *Mein Gott!* She vill drive me crazy yet! Qvestions! Qvestions! Alvays qvestions!"

He talked with Willa's mother and told her that her daughter was learning nothing about the piano. After she had heard his story, Virginia Cather said that although Willa was not learning to play like his other pupils, she was learning a great deal by hearing him play and by asking questions. She asked him to begin coming twice as often as he had previously.

So to this group of people who helped Willa Cather's

mind and spirit grow must be added her mother. Virginia Cather allowed her daughter's personality the freedom to develop as it would, neither forcing it nor trying to contain it within a narrow framework. No matter what pressures the town exerted to make her conform, and no matter how much scorn and disapproval she suffered when she refused, Willa Cather could always find within her own family and circle of acquaintances encouragement to be herself. The result was a strength of will and a steadiness of purpose which were to help her become an artist.

four

Not all of Willa's days after she moved to town were spent
in serious study. The country was still important to her
and she loved exploring it with her two brothers. Often
they would hitch up the buggy and drive out to the
Divide—as the broad plateau between the Little Blue and
Republican rivers was called—to visit the old Bohemian,
Swedish, and German friends they had known on the
homestead. With her father in the farm-loan business,
farming was still a major topic of conversation in her
home. She could discuss every phase of it with these old
friends.

There was plenty of time for play, too, all of it colored
and shaped by her fertile imagination. The move into

Red Cloud brought a new segment of the countryside within her range: the river two miles south of town. The Republican was a shallow stream, studded with sandbars and lined with wooded banks. Willa, her brothers, and her friends swam and canoed there, but its chief attraction for them was its opportunities for make-believe. Their familiarity with *Treasure Island* and the other writings of Robert Louis Stevenson and those of Mark Twain, coupled with their youthful imaginations, made the river a place of romance. A large sandbar became their pirate island and Willa Cather gave special names to parts of it—the Silvery Beeches, the Uttermost Desert, the Salt Marshes, the Huge Fallen Tree.

The river became an even more fascinating place to them when they learned about the Spanish explorer, Coronado, in school. Most scholars believed that the Spaniard had not followed the Republican River as far north as Red Cloud in his search for the seven golden cities, but only a few years before the Cathers came to Nebraska, a homesteader had found two ancient Spanish stirrups in his pasture a few miles northwest of Red Cloud. Willa and her playmates were certain that the explorer and his men had marched over the same ground on which they played then. That belief deepened the mystery and romance the river held for them.

Willa had been ill with what was probably polio before the family moved to town, and she was supposed to walk with a crutch. However, she grew impatient with it, threw it away, and was soon walking and running as well as the other children.

Her first playmate when the Cathers moved into Red Cloud was Mary Miner, whose family lived nearby. Mary, whose father ran a general merchandise store, brought Willa a bottle of perfume in a red plush slipper as a welcoming gift. Mary's sisters and her brother and the

Cather children formed friendships that lasted the rest of their lives.

She loved to visit the Miner Brothers' Store with Mary. When no one was looking, they would sneak upstairs to the candy barrel and help themselves to their favorite candy—a small cylinder coated with various flavors, white inside, and in the very center a red rose, a green shamrock, or a red-white-and-blue top hat. If the big barrel was nearly empty, one of them would take off her shoes and stockings and climb in to get the candy. It was an adventure filled with suspense, for discovery meant instant banishment from the store.

Whenever Willa could, she tiptoed into the Miner house to listen to Mary at her piano practice, and then coaxed her to play all the songs she knew. When Mary grew tired, but was too polite to say so, she began to play "Pompinette," a number Willa Cather hated. It was the only thing that would send her home.

Mary's eldest sister, Carrie, worked as bookkeeper at her father's store. Because Carrie was older, Willa liked being around her. Willa raised so many questions that Mr. Miner, exasperated, asked Carrie why she spent so much time with "that child." But Carrie did not consider Willa a nuisance and enjoyed talking with her. Because Carrie was old enough to be considered an adult, she was always welcome in Willa's attic room, the Rose Bower, which was off limits to the other children. Closing the door behind them, Willa would say, "Well, now, what then?" and off the two girls would go into one of their endless arguments. Willa was fond of arguing either in formal debate or otherwise.

Mrs. Miner had been born in Norway, the daughter of an oboe soloist with the Royal Norwegian Orchestra. As a child, she attended rehearsals and concerts and throughout her life she retained her interest in music. She played operatic selections on her piano and she was one through whom Willa first became acquainted with fine music, which was to give her so many hours of pleasure throughout her life.

Willa Cather put Mrs. Miner in *My Ántonia,* the only time she ever drew a portrait of an actual person in any of her novels. She had never forgotten how Mrs. Miner's white hands looked as she played the piano, and Willa described them in the book.

Carrie Miner was astonished: "Willie, what a strange thing to remember! Where do you store such things?"

Willa replied, "When I was writing about it, it came right out of the ink bottle."

Willa did not care to play with dolls and dress them. She preferred to dress herself up and playact, either at home or in public. Her first successes as an actress came soon after the Cathers left the homestead and moved into Red Cloud. Sunday School programs gave her frequent opportunities to perform. One of her most popular readings was Longfellow's poem *Hiawatha.* During this recitation she held a bow and arrow and, at the proper moment, fell to one knee and shot into an imaginary forest.

Her cousin, Bess Seymore, who lived with the Cathers, served as her model and instructor. Bess was generally chosen to play the lead in the community plays. Rehearsals were frequently held in the Cather house where Willa watched and listened with absorption. Before she was thirteen, she was plotting and directing plays of her own.

Many of her plays were not performed on a stage but were enacted wherever the children happened to be playing. Willa Cather had a way of making her dramas so realistic that Irene, the youngest of the Miner children, was not sure how much was truth and how much was make-believe. One evening at supper she recounted the exciting events of their day, mixing fact with fantasy until her father exclaimed, "I think the Miner children and the Cather children should be separated for awhile or they'll all grow up to be incurable liars."

Willa presented her first formal play in the Miner home before an audience of friends and family. The entrance hall was used as dressing room, the parlor as stage, and the dining room as auditorium. In the open arch between parlor and dining room Willa and the Miner girls hung sliding curtains.

The play, based on a currently popular story, "Dr. Allen," was such a success that a few months later the children presented another at the Opera House to raise money for victims of the 1888 blizzard. They asked Peorianna Sill and Will O'Brien, a clerk in the Miner's store, for advice and assistance. Mr. O'Brien had studied Shakespearean roles in Boston and New York, was expert in speech and diction, and had already taught some of the children to dance. Mrs. Miner made the costumes.

The play the girls chose was "Beauty and the Beast." Margie Miner was Beauty, Mary Miner was the Beast, and Willa Cather, dressed in a man's suit and hat and wearing a waxed mustache, was the father. The performance was an astonishing success. When Mary, as the Beast, came lumbering on stage in costume and bear's mask, chanting a weird melody and swaying to its rhythm, the scene was so realistic a nervous woman screamed.

Mrs. Newhouse, a German woman who ran a local store, asked Carrie after the play, "Where did you get dat boy?"

Carrie laughed. "That wasn't a boy. That was Willie Cather."

Mrs. Newhouse shook her head. "Dat not Villie Cader. He valk like boy. He talk like boy. Dat not Villie Cader."

The proceeds from the play amounted to forty dollars, which was distributed to needy families in the form of groceries.

Half a dozen times each winter, a traveling stock company arrived in Red Cloud to present plays at the Opera House. Each visit meant a glamorous week for Willa and her friends. The excitement began even before the actors arrived. An advance man would suddenly appear and post bills advertising the plays in the windows of stores, on the sides of barns, and on the lumberyard fence. The children would stand for an hour after school studying those posters, the names of the plays, and the nights on which each would be given.

If a company arrived on the night train, the children always walked to the depot to see the train come in. They watched with fascination as the actors alighted, paced the platform while their baggage was being sorted, and then rode off in the bus to the hotel.

These were only preludes to the magic that was to come. It was the performances themselves that carried Willa into another world, a land of romance and adventure. She continued to be stagestruck for years, and it was her columns of dramatic criticism, written for Lincoln newspapers while she was attending the state university there, that brought the name of Willa Cather before the national public for the first time.

Her imagination was never idle. When Dr. G. E. McKeeby, the Cather family doctor, was elected mayor of Red Cloud and Charles Cather became an alderman, thirteen-year-old Willa decided to enter politics too. She and her playmates founded Sandy Point along the south fence of the Cather yard in the shade of cottonwood and wild plum trees. The town was built of packing boxes obtained from Miner Brothers' Store, and Willa persuaded her father to gravel a strip than ran the entire length of the yard: Sandy Point's Main Street. Each child chose his business and made a sign for his store.

Willa campaigned for mayor and won, which was not surprising since the whole idea of the box town had been hers. She established the mayor's office halfway up Main Street and began her duties by calling the citizens of Sandy Point to a meeting to discuss building a bridge over a ditch on the north side of the Cather yard. It was a worthwhile project because Margie Miner was recovering from a bout with polio and had to be pulled about in a wagon. The idea was endorsed and Willa's brothers, Roscoe and Douglas, soon had the bridge completed.

The town had a varied assortment of businesses. Mary Miner ran a candy shop and kept it stocked with taffy. Jessica Cather kept the post office and also ran the Fair Store. A piano box served as a hotel and Margie Miner's store sold whistles, tablets, and pencils. The millinery shop, operated by Irene Miner and Laura McNitt from next door, was a two-story building. Both girls were so small that they could climb into the upper box. They believed the second floor provided the privacy necessary for trying on hats.

Some of the merchandise was donated by the mothers and fathers. The remainder was bought by the children with their own money. Within Sandy Point, however, the only money used was the Confederate bills which the Cather family had used for packing dishes when they moved from Virginia.

In addition to her duties as mayor, Willa took on the job of editing their play newspaper, *The Sandy Point News*. The experience seemed to light no fire within her to become a writer. In fact she made a firm decision not long afterward to become a surgeon. This decision stemmed from several circumstances. A bag of medical instruments arrived at the Cather home along with the other personal belongings of an uncle who had died not long after becoming a doctor. The instruments strengthened Willa's interest in zoology which she shared with Mr. Ducker. Her friendships with Doctor McKeeby and

Willa Cather, New York, 1927.
Photographed by Edward Steichen

Willa Cather from a photograph by W. W. Wilson

Willa Cather in 1902
at the beginning of her career

The portrait of Willa Cather by Leon Bakst
which hangs in the Omaha, Nebraska, Public Library

Willa Cather in 1921. Photographed by E. A. Hoppé

Willa Cather on vacation in New Hampshire in 1923

Doctor Damerell also stimulated her interest in the m[edi]cal profession. She often went on calls with Do[ctor] Damerell and once she gave chloroform to a boy wh[ose] leg the doctor had to amputate. Doctor Cook, w[ho] operated the Red Cloud pharmacy, was a friend of Will[a] too. He allowed her to work in his store and take her p[ay] in books, games, and a magic lantern.

Using the new instruments, she began dissecting toad[s] and cats to study their circulatory systems. Many people were shocked and regarded her with stern disapproval. To make matters worse, she began dressing like a boy. When her brother Jim was born, her mother was too sick to take care of Willa's long hair, so Willa simply went to the barber and had it cut off. In addition to sporting her boyish haircut, she began to wear boy's clothes—shirts, ties, hats; she even carried a cane on occasion. Her family and friends had always called her "Willie," but now she preferred "Will." Most of the books in her small personal library she inscribed "Wm Cather Jr." If someone really wished to please her, he called her "Doctor Will."

A page in the autograph album of a friend reveals a great deal about the Willa Cather of this period. The page presented a list of statements to be completed. Opposite *Favorite Flower* Willa Cather wrote "cauliflower." Opposite *My Idea of Perfect Happiness* she wrote "amputating limbs." Her *Idea of Real Misery* was "doing fancy work." The qualification she most desired in a husband was "lamb-like meekness." One of the statements read: *"There is always some one person, or thing, for which we have an attachment exceeding all other endearments in intensity. With me it is for————."* In the blank Willa Cather wrote "Books." She declared her chief ambition in life was to be a doctor and she signed the page "Wm Cather, M.D."

One of the statements asked for the trait which she

least respected in another person. Her reply was "lack of nerve"—a trait she herself was not burdened with. Her determination to follow her own path instead of the one the town insisted was proper for a young woman earned her some sharp criticism. Many people thought her queer and declared that no good would come of her.

She found a chance to reply to some of her critics in her high-school commencement address. Her topic was "Superstition versus Investigation," and in the speech she defended her dissecting cats and toads to study their circulatory systems. She maintained that it is the sacred right of man to investigate and that scientific investigation was the hope of the age. Even the local newspaper called it a "masterpiece of oratory," although the article had no glowing words to say about her future as it had for the two boys who were being graduated with her.

Charles Cather preferred that his daughter teach a year or two before she entered the state university, but Willa wanted to enroll the next fall. Her mother backed her up and her father gave in as he nearly always did to his precocious daughter. Willa began preparations for what she believed would be her education to become a physician and surgeon.

five

Willa discovered that she could not go directly into the university. She had not been able to earn enough science credits in the Red Cloud High School. Because many of the smaller schools throughout the state did not at that time offer all the courses necessary for entrance into the university, a preparatory school had been established in Lincoln. Most of its courses were taught by members of the university faculty. The Latin School, as it was called, offered a two-year program to enable students to make up their deficiencies. Willa Cather was enrolled in the senior year.

One of her fellow students recalls that while the preparatory class in Greek was waiting that first morning for the instructor to begin the lesson, the door opened and a head, short-haired and straw-hatted, appeared. A deep masculine voice asked if this was where the class in elementary Greek was meeting. Someone near the door replied that it was, and as the newcomer opened the door wide to reveal a girl's figure and skirts, the entire class burst into laughter. Willa Cather, unperturbed by the laughter, quietly took her place.

In Lincoln she roomed at the home of Kate Hastings, a friend of the family whom Willa called "Aunt Kate." She took her meals at the best boardinghouse in town. Her room was heated by a coal stove for which she carried the coal herself, up two flights of stairs. One of the walls she covered with a large map of Rome which she bought with her pocket money.

Here in this rather bleak room she applied herself to her studies. At the end of the year that was to prepare her for entrance into the university, she still believed that science was the field she was most interested in. Yet she had not lost her love for the Latin and Greek classics and when she enrolled in the university, she registered as a classical student. The only science course she chose was freshman chemistry.

Something happened that first winter that pushed her interest in science into the background permanently. Her instructor in English, Professor Ebenezer Hunt, assigned a long theme on the topic "The Personal Characteristics of Thomas Carlyle." Professor Hunt was always alert for signs of originality in writing and he found them in the paper Willa Cather turned in. As a matter of fact, he was so impressed with her theme that he arranged for its appearance in the local newspaper, the *State Journal,* without telling its author.

When Willa Cather saw her theme in print, and read the editor's compliments on it, her ambition to become a doctor was put away forever. Perhaps she would have found her way to art by some other route. She had from childhood translated everything in her life—books, people, places—into imaginative experience. But it was the encouragement and stimulation of this first success that seem to have shown her how this basic part of her nature could be put to vital use.

When she finished prep school and entered the university, she chose courses that would offer exposure to great literature and the wisdom of great civilizations. That meant further study of the Latin and Greek classics and English literature. Her knowledge of the latter was so much greater than that of the average student that she was allowed to substitute advanced courses for those normally required.

At the beginning of her sophomore year, in the autumn of 1892, she became one of the editors of the undergraduate literary magazine, *The Hesperian*. She was its largest contributor, writing verse, criticism, dialogues, satirical sketches of students, and stories.

Her first published story had appeared six months earlier, on May 21, 1892 in a Boston literary weekly called *The Mahogany Tree*. She republished it in *The Hesperian* in November, shortly after she became an editor. From that time on her stories, probably written as assignments for her class in English composition, appeared frequently. Many of the elements in her later novels about Nebraska were present in these early works. There is the deep concern over the plight of immigrants in a society that has no sympathy for their problems. There are the alarm and dislike at the pressure a community exerts on a person who does not mold himself to its standards.

During her first two years in college Willa studied hard, rising early in the morning and working far into the night. In time she grew increasingly impatient with the conventional methods her Latin and Greek professors used to teach the classics. She was irritated beyond endurance by the dry, mechanical methods of Professor Lucius A. Sherman, her English literature teacher. His interest was in deep analysis of words and sounds, in insignificant details. There came a time when Willa Cather could control her exasperation no longer. In a written test, after answering a long list of questions that she considered ridiculous, she replied to the question "What did the noble matron Volumnia say then?" with, "The noble matron Volumnia then said 'Bow-wow.'"

Her arguments with Professor Sherman in class were frequent and he told her in so many words that she would never amount to anything.

Willa had no intention of becoming a scholar and was not interested in the small details of the classics but in the great sweep of ideas they offered. She began to spend more and more time reading on her own, exploring authors who had special value for her personal life and who could show her how fine fiction and poetry should be written.

Among the authors she chose to read was Flaubert, whose novel *Madame Bovary* she often carried with her. She also read Maupassant and Ibsen and the younger Dumas. Having been acquainted with some of Robert Louis Stevenson's writings since childhood, she began to read all of them now—not so much for the stories as to study Stevenson's style. She bought a complete set of his books, paying for it at the rate of a dollar a month, and continued to read him throughout her life.

In Lincoln, as in Red Cloud, she formed friendships with people who aided her growth as a person and as an artist. Mr. and Mrs. Goudy, old friends, were there of course. James H. Canfield, chancellor of the University of Nebraska, was always alert for any student who showed rare gifts; he discovered Willa Cather through his son James, who was in her class. She became one of the family and formed a friendship with the chancellor's daughter, Dorothy, that lasted throughout their lives. Dorothy Canfield became a famous writer, too. Mrs. Canfield, a highly talented individual herself, rejoiced in any young person who spelled Art with a capital A, as Willa Cather did. Mrs. Canfield's broad reading in French literature and her acquaintance with many French artists were important to Willa.

Another family who more or less adopted Willa as one of their own was the Geres. Charles H. Gere was editor of the *State Journal*, the newspaper that had printed Willa Cather's essay on Carlyle. The Geres had three daughters and when one of them, Mariel, invited Willa Cather to their home, she warned her mother that she was bringing home a girl who was rather masculine. After Mrs. Gere had met Willa, she exclaimed, "She's not at all masculine!" In time she persuaded Willa to let her hair grow and to put aside the boyish clothes for soft blouses and skirts.

Willa had been in Lincoln several years before she met Dr. Julius Tyndale and his sister, Mrs. Emma Tyndale Westermann. Mrs. Westermann and her husband, William, spoke German fluently and their family life, so deeply marked by European culture, meant a great deal to Willa. They offered her, in a more highly developed form, the same values she had found in the home of Mr. and Mrs. Charles Wiener in Red Cloud.

Doctor Tyndale's friendship was particularly important to her. He had entered the Civil War as a drummer and, after becoming a surgeon, had served with the Seventh Cavalry. His interest in music and letters was as great as his interest in science. He took Willa to many concerts in Lincoln and told her stories about the literary and musical worlds of the East Coast. His opinions about art became an important element in her growth. Just before her graduation from the university, he helped arrange a trip for her to Chicago for a week of opera. Her friend Mary L. Jones, acting librarian at the university, accompanied her. The excitement and stimulation of the city by day and the opera at night were too much for her. During her last evening of music she fell asleep even though the opera, Meyerbeer's *The Huguenots,* was a lively one, its music punctuated by the roll of many drums. She returned to Lincoln ill from exhaustion.

Her fellow students knew her as a high-spirited, self-confident girl who threw herself into college activities with great energy and enthusiasm. Being interested in drama as always, she both directed and acted in school plays. But the self she displayed to the world was not the whole picture. The other part of Willa Cather was groping for something she felt inside herself. Years later her heroine in *The Song of the Lark,* Thea Kronborg, who was destined to become a great opera star, went through the same groping period. Willa Cather wrote of her, "It was as if she had an appointment to meet the rest of herself sometime, somewhere. It was moving to meet her, and she was moving to meet it." She might have been describing her own experience.

Willa was aware of the power within herself, but she did not know where it would lead or how far it would take her.

The summer of 1893, between her sophomore and junior years at the university, was a disastrous one for the farmers and the businessmen of the state. For several years crops had not been good because of drought. That summer a hot wind burned up the new corn crop in three days. The Red Cloud bank failed and although Willa's father lost no money when it closed its doors, many of the men who owed him money did lose. He himself had bought a great deal of land which he had mortgaged. The interest and taxes on that land were mounting and he had no money coming in.

It was not easy for Charles to support his large family at this time. Roscoe and Douglas began teaching school in order to help out at home. Willa herself began writing literary and dramatic criticism that autumn for Mr. Gere's paper, the *State Journal*, at a dollar a column. Not only was she able to pay most of her expenses this way, but it was excellent experience for her. Any writer needs to write hundreds of thousands of words before he can write well. Willa wrote a surprisingly large number of columns those next two years and by the time she was graduated from college, she was a professional writer though not yet an artist.

A study of her book reviews reveals her own artistic aims. In one she said, "The further the world advances, the more it becomes evident that an author's only safe course is to cling to the skirts of his art, forsaking all others, and keep unto her as long as they two shall live. . . . Other men may think and believe and argue, but he must create."

Yet she knew that at twenty she had not lived enough to write the kind of fiction she wanted to write. She would have to ripen slowly as a field of wheat ripens.

It was her reviews of plays that attracted the most attention. She was merciless toward a poor play or an inferior performance. Second-rate dramatic companies began to tremble long before they reached Lincoln. An editorial in the *State Journal*, in which her columns appeared, observed that "many an actor of national reputation wondered on coming to Lincoln what would appear next morning from the pen of the meat-ax young girl of whom all of them had heard. Miss Cather did not stand in awe of the greatest actors, but set each one in his place with all the authority of a veteran metropolitan critic."

Some people believed she roasted more than she praised, but not all of what she wrote was critical. She was generous with her praise when a performance moved her and met her exacting standards.

Always a lover of books and drama, Willa Cather enjoyed her newspaper work, but the exhausting schedule began to take its toll. After a day filled with classes and study, she would spend the evening at the theater, then go over to the newspaper office and write her review of the play. Often it was one or two o'clock in the morning when she got home. In June, 1895, she was graduated and went home to Red Cloud. She wrote back to Mrs. Goudy in Lincoln that she was dead-tired, body and brain. She expected to enjoy a rest among her family, but she found the period that followed to be the most trying she had ever lived through.

six

Willa Cather found that, as Thomas Wolfe later said, "You can't go home again." Red Cloud was not the same and neither was she. Some of her older friends had died; others had moved away. She tried to resume her friendships with those who remained, but the old, close ties of childhood had been broken. That is not to say that these childhood friendships were broken; Willa Cather kept many throughout her life. But experience had changed her, broadened her intellect, opened new windows in her mind. She was dismayed to find that she no longer felt the old contentment she used to feel at home.

She spent much of that summer of 1895 in Lincoln, writing play reviews for the *State Journal*. In August she was hired as associate editor for the *Courier,* another Lincoln newspaper. For reasons unknown she remained with that paper only until November, when she returned to the *State Journal,* taking with her "The Passing Show," as she called her column.

In January she returned to Red Cloud and spent the remainder of the winter there, although she continued to make frequent visits to Lincoln to attend plays and write reviews. She also found time to write a short story, "On the Divide," which was published in a national magazine, the *Overland Monthly.*

By now Willa found herself in an uncomfortable position. Great things had been prophesied for her, but she seemed to be getting nowhere. She had been described in Nebraska newspapers as a literary woman of distinction whose dramatic criticism compared favorably with that of the Chicago papers. Mrs. Elia W. Peattie, a columnist for the Omaha *World Herald* and a nationally published fiction writer, described Willa Cather as "a young woman with a genius for literary expression. . . . If there is a woman in Nebraska newspaper work who is destined to win a reputation for herself, that woman is Willa Cather. She has great capacity for study, and is sure to grow from year to year in knowledge of her work and in felicity of style. . . ."

Willa was aware of these predictions for her future and felt, probably quite correctly, that many people in Red Cloud expected her to become a dazzling success in the writing field with short stories or perhaps a brilliant novel. For her part she longed to become instantly famous and force those who had always disapproved of her to eat crow. She knew, however, that to write as she wanted to write, she would have to travel and see something of the world. She wrote to friends bewailing what she called her "bitter exile" and referring to Red Cloud as Siberia. She yearned to escape the stagnation she felt there and to go someplace where there were music, drama, and art. To do this would take money that she did not have.

During the winter Herbert Bates, one of her former English instructors at the university, resigned and recommended that she be named in his place. She knew that her age and her sex were against her. She also knew that the head of the English department, Lucius Sherman, disliked her intensely because of her open contempt for his teaching methods. She enlisted friends in Lincoln in support to her application, but she was not surprised when she failed to get the job.

Spring came and still she suffered her "exile." It was bitter frustration for a girl who not only had the word of others that she was destined for great things but felt within herself the power to accomplish them.

At last an opportunity came. During one of her visits to the Gere family in Lincoln she had met Charles Axtell, a businessman from Pittsburgh, Pennsylvania. He was founding a new magazine and, aware of her extraordinary ability as a writer, he offered her a position in the editorial office of his magazine the *Home Monthly*. Willa Cather accepted at once and by the end of June she had left Red Cloud for Pittsburgh.

As far as her development as a writer is concerned, her job on the staff of the *Home Monthly* was of little value. It was a dull magazine that presented nothing more exciting than articles on flowers, babies, fashions, Christian Endeavor, and the pleasures of bicycle riding.

It was not long before Willa Cather was managing editor in everything but name, with only a stenographer to help her. She wrote friends back home that she had never worked so hard in her life. She read manuscripts and proof, worked in the hot composing room until late at night as the magazine was put together, and wrote articles and fillers. The responsibility was so great that when she finally got to bed, she dreamed about the magazine all night.

She felt frustrated because she had little time to write stories and when she did, they were shaped to fit the sentimental tone of the magazine. In her college themes she had been free to explore the talent which lay within her. In her magazine work she lacked that freedom. She knew that life did not always provide happy endings, that good did not always triumph over evil as the stories in the *Home Monthy* would have had its readers believe. Yet she needed the job and it gave her pleasure to prove to the doubters back in Red Cloud that she could succeed in a big Eastern city.

She found Pittsburgh stimulating even if her job was not. She loved its hills and rivers and plumes of gas flame, even its coal-smeared face. It hummed with industrial activity. Fortunes were made in steel and oil, coal and gas. The men who made them were pioneers in their own way and Willa had tremendous admiration for them. Unlike the silver kings in Nevada and Colorado, whose idea of art was the building of huge, ugly homes with fancy bathrooms, the steel kings of Pittsburgh were donating money for museums and concert halls. Grimy Pittsburgh was becoming one of America's centers of culture.

Willa escaped from her work and the drabness of her boardinghouse by making full use of these cultural facilities. At the new Carnegie Institute she found more books than had ever been available to her in Red Cloud and Lincoln. At Carnegie Hall she heard Victor Herbert conduct the symphony orchestra and met artists and composers. There was also the Pittsburgh stock company, which presented a new play every week.

In Pittsburgh as always she found her place in a circle of brilliant and talented people ranging from actresses to the chief librarian of the Carnegie Library, Edwin Hatfield Anderson. She went regularly to the home of another librarian, George Seibel, whose house showed the European influence. With him she read the French classics and improved her French. She became so good a friend of the family that she was present to help them trim their Christmas tree for each of the ten years she lived in Pittsburgh. During the trimming she always munched the needles of the tree and declared them a delicacy. According to Mr. Seibel, she would sometimes "voice regret that she was not a boa constrictor, who could feed full of Christmas evergreen and then curl up luxuriously under the tree to purr in rivalry with our cat."

Willa realized almost immediately after going to work on the *Home Monthly* that she would not be happy there. She began investigating the possibilities of finding work on one of the city's newspapers. At the end of her first year on the magazine she went home to Red Cloud for a vacation. From there she sent in her resignation. The magazine was going under new management, which provided her with an appropriate excuse to resign. A few weeks later she was hired by the Pittsburgh *Daily Leader*, the largest evening newspaper in Pennsylvania, at a salary of seventy-five dollars a month.

Her job consisted of the editing and rewriting of news which came in through the office telegraph, as well as copyreading and headline writing. It was drudgery of a sort, but it was better than her job had been on the *Home Monthly*. Here at least she did not have to write what she considered trash. News writing, however, was not satisfying to Willa. She was happier writing columns of dramatic criticism, which she had been doing for the *Daily Leader* even while working on the *Home Monthly*. She continued those columns after she became a member of the *Leader*'s editorial staff and was as merciless with poor plays and inferior acting as she had been back in Lincoln. She had not yet learned that criticism need not be heavy-handed, that a light touch can express disapproval as effectively as a mallet blow. She still used words like "awful" and "terrible" in describing plays she did not like, but she was learning.

In reality Willa's interests more often lay in the performers than in the play. Even second-rate actors lived in a world of artistic standards and endeavor and this was the world in which Willa herself belonged. She visited them backstage and in one instance became a good friend of one of them. Lizzie Hudson Collier was leading lady in the Pittsburgh stock company. She was a woman with a warm heart and generous nature. One night Willa was feverish and hoarse from a severe cold when she stopped by Mrs. Collier's dressing room backstage after a performance. The actress insisted on taking Willa home with her, put her to bed in her own room and nursed her for several days until she was well again.

It is not through Willa Cather's writing of dramatic criticism that one can obtain the picture of her as a maturing personality and artist. This stage of her growth is revealed in the series of columns she sent back to Nebraska which appeared first in the *State Journal* and later in the Lincoln *Courier*. She continued to call this column "The Passing Show" and in it she wrote about the arts and about the personalities who practiced them. She discovered A. E. Housman's poetry and shared her elation with her Nebraska readers. She discussed John Philip Sousa's music and told of her visits with Rudyard Kipling and many other famous people: She was an unabashed hero-worshiper. In addition to the accounts of the famous people she met and talked to, she included discussions of realism in the novel, of dramatic and lyric poetry, of the art of the actor and of the playwright.

When she first heard Dvořák's symphony *From the New World,* she wrote, "Before you stretch the empty, hungry plains of the middle west. Limitless prairies, full of the peasantry of all nations of Europe . . . and it seems as though from each of those far scattered lights that at night mark the dwellings of these people of the plains, there comes the song of a homesick heart."

Walter Damrosch came to Pittsburgh every year and presented Wagnerian opera for a week. Willa attended every performance and wrote about them in her columns. Of Wagner's music she observed that it "is not perhaps so effective as elsewhere" since "we are all so used to the noise of the iron mills."

Then as always she had no intellectual interest in music. Rather it was an emotional experience for her; and it greatly influenced her own imaginative processes; it quickened the flow of her ideas and suggested new forms and associations.

Those evenings spent at Carnegie Hall and the opera were most important to Willa Cather's future as a novelist. The great musicians she met there interested her not only as musicians but as individuals who had become artists through long discipline and firmness of purpose. She admired their "indefinable air of achievement." They provided her with an example to follow in the pursuit of her own art. One day she would write a novel, *The Song of the Lark,* which would be a study of the growth and development of a great singer.

She began to travel beyond Pittsburgh, going to New York to attend Broadway plays, visiting Washington, D.C. These trips and her increasing desire to become an artist made her job more and more distasteful to her. Newspaper work left her little time to write fiction. What stories she did write and place in various magazines revealed no improvement over those she had written in college. The fact that magazines were buying her stories was encouraging, however, and she began to search for a way to free herself from newspaper work.

In 1901 she left the Pittsburgh *Leader* and took a teaching position at Central High School. Her first year in teaching convinced her that the change had been wise. She taught only three or four hours a day and had a theme reader to assist her. At last she had time to write. She took her teaching duties seriously, though, and was well liked by her students. They were struck by her informal Western manner and by her voice, which was unusually deep for a woman. She believed that she was more successful as a teacher than she had been as a news writer and drama critic. As a matter of fact, it never gave her any pleasure to recall her newspaper work. Although she used every other part of her life in her novels and stories, journalism never figured in her writing. It had been only a means to an end. It had taken her out of the Midwest and set her down in the culture-rich East.

seven

It was in 1901, the year Willa Cather began teaching, that she met a young woman who was to offer her a friendship that would enrich her life and who provided her with an environment that helped her become a creative writer.

Willa Cather met Isabelle McClung in Lizzie Hudson Collier's dressing room backstage at the Pittsburgh stock company. Miss McClung was the daughter of a Pittsburgh judge who was stern and dignified and moderately wealthy. She rebelled against the strictness of her home life and turned to the world of art. She was not an artist herself, but she possessed a complete understanding of the artist's efforts and goals. She recognized excellence instinctively and was immediately drawn to Willa.

Soon after their friendship was formed, Isabelle invited Willa to come to live in the McClung mansion. Willa had found life in a boardinghouse dreary and lonely; she was glad to accept. It was like a dream come true. She would be living in a house much like that of the Charles Wieners in Red Cloud or the Westermanns in Lincoln, a house filled with books and pictures and cultivated manners.

The McClung house was even more spacious and elegant than those others had been. Dorothy Canfield Fisher later remembered the McClung home as "a great rich house, with plenty of servants, and conducted in the lavish style of half a century ago. Isabelle was simply devoted to Willa always, and was sweet, warm-hearted and sincere—as well as very beautiful, at least I used to think her so, in a sumptuous sort of way. There was a good deal of stately entertaining carried on in the Mc-Clung house too, the many-coursed dinners of the most formal kind, which seemed picturesque (and they really were) to Willa."

Although Judge and Mrs. McClung welcomed Willa as their daughter's friend, they were not sure it was a good idea to invite her to make her home with them. Isabelle had her way, however, and Willa soon won them over. She was to be a member of their household for five years. There in a quiet room at the back of the house she found a calmness and a peace which allowed her to begin the serious writing she had been yearning to do.

Elizabeth Moorhead, who became a friend of Isabelle's and Willa's, describes how Willa appeared to her upon her first visit to the McClung house:

"Short, rather stocky in build, she had a marked directness of aspect. You saw at once that here was a person who couldn't easily be diverted from her chosen course. Pretty would indeed be a trivial word to describe a face that showed so much strength of character as hers, yet she was distinctly good-looking, with a clear, rosy skin, eyes of light gray and hair a dark brown brushed back from a low forehead—an odd and charming contrast in color. They were observant eyes, nothing escaped them. . . . She looked me straight in the face as she greeted me, and I felt her absolute frankness and honesty. She would never say anything she didn't mean. . . ."

Willa wrote evenings, weekends, and during school holidays. In the spring of 1902, when school let out, she and Isabelle made their first trip abroad together. Willa helped pay her expenses by writing a series of articles for the Lincoln *State Journal* describing her trip.

Going to Europe was in a sense a "homecoming" for Willa. She had been exposed to a smattering of European cultures through her friendships with the immigrants on the prairie, and with people like the Seibels and the Westermanns, through her introduction to French literature by Mrs. Charles Wiener, and through her reading of the Latin and Greek classics with Mr. Ducker. America was too young to have an old culture of its own and she had felt the lack sharply, especially during the years she had spent on the raw prairie. When she set foot in Europe, she was stirred mentally and emotionally.

In England she was thrilled to discover reminders that that country had once been a part of Imperial Rome, about which she had read with Mr. Ducker.

After traveling through the small towns on the west coast of Britain and spending five weeks in London, Willa and Isabelle crossed the Channel to France. It was Willa's journeys through this country that stirred her most. Always sensitive to landscape, she found that of France enchanting with its warmth and color, its people, and its buildings. She rejoiced in its food and wines and in its history. She made pilgrimages to the graves and monuments of the great writers of France whose work she had admired for so long—Flaubert, Maupassant, Balzac.

Here was life that was rooted in the centuries and

Willa, with her great love of the past, drank it in in great gulps, feeling her spirit grow and expand. Many years later, in her novel *Death Comes for the Archbishop,* she was to have Bishop Latour remark on tasting a soup: ". . . a soup like this is not the work of one man. It is the result of a constantly refined tradition. There are nearly a thousand years of history in this soup."

Although Willa Cather was to make several trips to Europe in her lifetime, none was to leave impressions as deep as these first ones.

In 1903, after her return to America, her first book was published. *April Twilights* was a volume of poems, most of which had been published previously in magazines. The twilights referred to belonged to Nebraska, not to Pittsburgh. In these poems there are echoes of Vergil and Horace, and also of A. E. Housman, the English poet she so much admired and whom she had visited while in England. One can find in them the subjects and moods that she was to use later in her novels. Publication of the book made her something of a celebrity among the teachers and pupils of Allegheny High, the school where she was then teaching.

A woman who met Willa during this period in her life, Ethel Jones Litchfield, remembered her as very busy with her teaching, her writing, and her friends. Yet she always found time for music and the theater. She liked in particular to attend chamber-music rehearsals in which Mrs. Litchfield, a talented pianist, participated with Pittsburgh's leading musicians. Frequently guest artists would be booked for concerts, among them a violinist, Jan Hambourg, who was later to marry Isabelle McClung and to whom Willa dedicated two of her novels.

She was writing short stories during this time, in the quiet room Isabelle had provided her, working slowly and carefully. Most of them were accepted by the better magazines such as *Lippincott's* and *McClure's*. There was so much interest shown by the public in these stories that she assembled them in a book which McClure, Phillips and Company published in 1905 under the title *The Troll Garden*.

Three of these stories presented artists in relationships with people of great wealth. Another three stories showed artists or persons of artistic temperament returning in defeat to the prairies where they had been reared. These latter stories arose from memories of her youth in Red Cloud, of her differentness and the intolerance and scorn it had aroused. Her attitude toward the people of these small prairie towns was still bitter. She was discovering that, as she had Thea Kronborg say in *The Song of the Lark*, "nothing that she would ever do . . . would seem important to them, and nothing they would ever do would seem important to her."

Publication of this book of short stories marked another turning point in Willa Cather's life. It was to take her from Pittsburgh to New York, where she entered the final phase of her literary apprenticeship.

eight

At the time *The Troll Garden* was published, one of the most respected magazines in the country was *McClure's*. It contained articles, exposés, and stories by some of the best writers in the United States and England. When its publisher, S. S. McClure, read the volume of Willa Cather's stories, he was so impressed that he came to Pittsburgh to meet her. Judge McClung invited him to dinner and afterward McClure had a talk with Willa. The result was that at the end of the school year, Willa resigned from the faculty of Allegheny High and moved to New York to go to work for *McClure's Magazine*.

The atmosphere within the editorial office of the magazine was electric, the pace hectic. At the center of the storm was S. S. McClure himself, a genius who spewed forth ideas faster than they could be developed. He was everywhere at once and his furious energy kept the place in a state of high tension. An idea would come to him in the night and he could scarcely wait for morning, when he would speed to the office and begin discussing it with each of his staff. His own office was at the rear and it often took him half the morning to get to it, pausing at each desk to explain his idea and to try to convince his staff that it was a good one. Some of his schemes were impracticable and the staff would then have to find ways to evade those assignments.

Many people found the frantic pace he set impossible to bear. Others recognized him for the extraordinary man he was and found deep satisfaction in working for him. Willa was one of the latter. She had great respect for creative people whether they were opening up a new country or editing a magazine. She found him unfailingly courteous to everyone, from staff writers to office boys. He never lost his temper and was in fact the gentlest of men. Yet when he had an idea, he wanted it acted upon at once. Willa had a way of disapproving his bad ideas without offending him, and the liking they felt for each other upon first meeting was never strained.

When she moved to New York, Willa chose an apartment in Greenwich Village on the South side of Washington Square. It was an old building with many inconveniences, including a shortage of baths. It was very different from the luxury she had enjoyed in the McClung household, but she liked living among the young artists and musicians and writers who occupied the other rooms. In a story she wrote years later, called "Coming, Aphrodite!", she recorded her delight in the beauty of Washington Square and her interest in the immigrant population that lived nearby.

Although it was her stories that first interested S. S. McClure in Willa Cather, he put her to work on a series of articles that were to take up two of the six years she spent with the magazine. A manuscript had turned up at *McClure's* telling the story of Mary Baker Eddy, founder of the Christian Science religion. Some of the disclosures in the articles were so startling that the most careful checking had to be done before the manuscript could be used in the magazine. S. S. McClure assigned Willa this task. She would have little time to give to her fiction writing; nevertheless, the assignment was to have the most profound effect on her development as an artist. Because of it she was to meet Sarah Orne Jewett.

Working on the series of articles meant that Willa had to go to Boston, where she lived for most of 1907 and part of 1908. It meant that she had to spend a great deal of time traveling about New England, interviewing many of Mary Baker Eddy's early associates, digging into records and checking the accuracy of every fact that went into the articles.

Willa lived at first in the old Parker House, a hotel that was a favorite of Charles Dickens's, during his trips to America. It was the kind of place Willa Cather loved—a fireplace in each bedroom, a large library filled with beautifully bound sets of many of the classics. Later she took an apartment on Chestnut Street.

She had one friend in Boston from the beginning. Ferris Greenslet, a book critic, had given *April Twilights* an excellent review and after Willa Cather had written to thank him, a cordial friendship developed between them. Later, through his influence, the house of Houghton Mifflin became the publishers of her first four novels.

An acquaintance with Louis Brandeis—later Justice Brandeis of the Supreme Court—and his wife soon grew into a firm friendship. From the first Louis Brandeis's intuition told him that within this squarely built young woman who glowed with life and intelligence lay the soul of an artist and that she was safe in allowing her talent to dominate her life. Willa was delighted to find that the Brandeises shared many of her tastes in music and literature. She thought Mrs. Brandeis was an ideal wife for her husband—handsome, intelligent, perceptive.

One day when Willa called on Mrs. Brandeis, the older woman told her she wished to take her to meet the widow of James T. Fields, who had been a publisher of the *Atlantic Monthly* magazine and a member of Ticknor and Fields, a publishing house.

When they arrived, they were given tea by a small fragile woman who, although she was nearly eighty, had kept her clear blue eyes and youthful gaiety. She had known most of the great artists of her time, and her house was filled with mementos of them. Charles Dickens had considered it "home" when he was in America. In one of the bedrooms upstairs Thackeray had written a part of *Henry Esmond*. Oliver Wendell Holmes had been a neighbor and had dropped in frequently. Henry Wadsworth Longfellow, Ralph Waldo Emerson, and Nathaniel Hawthorne all had been entertained there.

To Willa the house seemed a magic place where the past was as alive as the present. She would not have been surprised to see a great actor or writer of an earlier day suddenly appear in the long drawing room where Mrs. Fields held court. All her life Willa had yearned for the atmosphere she found in this house, an atmosphere wherein the arts and manners of an earlier time lingered with none of the dryness of the classroom but with a living, breathing presence.

Between Willa Cather and Mrs. Fields there was immediate liking. Willa had always liked elderly women, felt at ease with them, and enjoyed drawing on their vast store of experience. She was to call often at this house in the seven years Mrs. Fields had left to live and the older woman was to treat Willa more like a grandchild full of Midwestern energy in need of a little toning down.

Fruitful as her relationship with Mrs. Fields was to be, there was another woman in that long green drawing room who would have an even greater impact on her life. Sarah Orne Jewett, a New England writer, was Mrs. Fields's closest friend. She was to die sixteen months after that meeting and Willa was the last person to whom she gave her friendship.

Sarah Orne Jewett was twenty-five years older than Willa Cather, yet their backgrounds were strikingly similar. Each had grown up in a small town which she had loved and had had to watch decline. South Berwick, Maine, had been a thriving shipping and shipbuilding town until after the Civil War, when it began to fail. Red Cloud had withered from drought and depression. Both women had entered eagerly into the lives of their towns and had had their imaginations stirred by the interplay between the townsfolk and the people of the farms. Both had been tomboys, riding about the countryside and loving every tree in it. Each had been taken on long drives to lonely farmhouses by a country doctor. Each cherished a past that she believed was giving way to a present that was cheap and ugly.

Willa had long been an admirer of Miss Jewett's writing. For her part, the New England authoress, with her high-piled brown hair and brown eyes, her aristocratic manner, took a special interest in this young writer from the prairies, with her sparkling enthusiasm, her hint of rare ability, and her striking blue-gray eyes.

They met often after that at Mrs. Fields's house and at South Berwick, where Sarah Orne Jewett lived with her sister, Mary, in a house that had come down to them from their grandfather, a retired sea captain and shipbuilder.

Perhaps Miss Jewett yearned for a literary heir. At any rate she passed on to Willa Cather her own writing creed —the harmony, simplicity, and understatement of a mature prose style. She felt that Willa's creative talent was threatened by the editorial work she was doing at *McClure's*. She urged her in one of the many letters they exchanged to give up her job and find a quiet place to perfect her work. She had read the stories Willa had done recently for the magazine and could see in them no deepening of Willa's inward life, no ripening of her talent. She warned that time was running short for Willa, then thirty-five years old. If she was to become the artist that she seemed capable of becoming, she could afford to waste no more time.

Willa never forgot that letter. She was only too aware of the truth in it. She realized she was using her best years editing a magazine instead of developing as a writer. She knew the editing job was far too stimulating for someone of her temperament. People had always excited Willa. At *McClure's* she worked too close to them, had to meet too many of them. They used her up, exhausted her nervously. She once wrote to Mrs. Goudy in Lincoln that she found the world too big, that one got split up into too many different currents. Yet she could not quit her job. She needed her salary.

"What is so hard to find—though seemingly simple—as four walls within which one can write?" Willa Cather asked gloomily one evening of her friend, Elizabeth Shepley Sergeant. Their friendship had begun a short time earlier when Miss Sergeant brought to *McClure's* a manuscript she had written, hoping to get it published.

Willa's father wanted to build her a small studio in his backyard in Red Cloud, but she knew she couldn't write there. The Divide would exercise its magnetic pull on her as it always did when she went home. She would be out riding and visiting all the time and get no writing done.

To write, she said, one needed to be dull, emptied of all stimulation. One needed to be completely alone or protected by someone who knew what it was all about as Isabelle McClung had protected her in Pittsburgh. Her New York apartment was too cramped, too near the office for her to be able to relax and write.

She wanted to write not of life, but wanted life itself. Yet in order to do this she knew she must cut herself off from it. Among others things it meant forgoing a husband and children and dedicating herself to art.

Soon after she completed the articles on Mary Baker Eddy, Willa sailed for Europe with Isabelle McClung. On her return to New York she was made managing editor of *McClure's*. By this time she had made up her mind to save every dollar she could for the quiet place Sarah Orne Jewett had told her she must find if she were to become the artist she hoped to be.

As managing editor Willa continued to read incoming manuscripts. This experience was to have a strong effect on her own later practice of writing fiction. More than ninety percent of the stories she read were depressingly conventional, containing no surprises, no freshness. The few unconventional manuscripts were so crudely written as to be unpublishable. It seemed to her that a true writer would allow his subject to take command of him, to choose its own form. For his own part, she felt, a writer must ready himself for this by serving an honest apprenticeship and learning well the writing craft.

Her own apprenticeship had been a long one and now she allowed a subject from her past to work its way to the surface of her mind and choose its own form. The result was a story she called "The Enchanted Bluff." Strictly speaking, it is not a story, for it has no plot, no action, no conflict. Rather it is a sketch that tells of six boys who camp overnight on a sandbar in a prairie river and discuss an enchanted bluff in the Southwest which someone they know has seen. The enchanted bluff is supposed to contain the remains of an Indian tribe that had been isolated in prehistoric times by a landslide. More than that, however, the sketch leads one into the spirit land to which Spanish explorers had come in search of gold. It was a piece out of Willa Cather's own past when she used to play on the sandbars in the Republican River with her brothers and friends and dream of the days when Coronado and his men had perhaps marched through that very valley.

"The Enchanted Bluff," which appeared in *Harper's*, was the best thing she had ever done. It was the type of writing Sarah Orne Jewett had urged her to do. It is not known whether Miss Jewett ever had the pleasure of reading it, for she died before it was published. Nevertheless, Willa Cather had shown what could be expected of her in the future.

nine

Willa Cather's next piece of work, following "The Enchanted Bluff," was a short novel called *Alexander's Bridge*, which appeared in *McClure's* in installments. In her later years, Willa Cather was a severe critic of that first novel, an imitation of the style of Henry James, whom Willa Cather admired very much. It was the story of a man who built great bridges and of the conflicts within his personal life. This was not the subject matter Willa Cather knew best. She was not drawing upon the rich fund of material in her past in which she was most at home. As a result the novel was rather shallow and artificial—good for a first novel, perhaps, but falling short of Willa Cather's true potential.

In the fall of 1911, Willa arranged for several months' leave of absence from *McClure's*. She spent the remainder of that autumn and the following winter in Cherry Valley, New York, where she shared a house with Isabelle Mc-Clung. She produced two stories during that time, "The Bohemian Girl" and "Alexandra." In both she was writing of the Nebraska prairie, a region she knew from her past but one that was strange to the public. She liked "The Bohemian Girl" very much and so did her friend Elizabeth Shepley Sergeant, to whom she showed it, but she was certain no magazine would want to publish it. Miss Sergeant's praise and delight convinced her of its merit and she took it to *McClure's*.

Cameron Mackenzie, who had taken over as managing editor in her absence, astounded her with his reaction to it: He offered her $750 for it. When she had recovered herself, she told him that she knew far better than he that no story was worth more than $500 to *McClure's*. Mackenzie didn't agree and made her promise to take even more money for the next story.

The other story, "Alexandra," did not satisfy her and she did not offer it for publication.

It is not clear whether Willa resigned from *McClure's* at this time or merely requested a longer leave of absence. At any rate shortly afterward, early in 1912, she left on her first visit to the Southwest. Douglass Cather, her brother, worked for the Santa Fe railroad and lived in Winslow, Arizona, where he shared a small house with another railroad man, named Tooker. When they were children, Willa and her brothers had often talked of one of their favorite dreams: exploring the Southwest together. The romance lent by the ancient Indian civilizations and the explorations of the Spaniards had always excited their imaginations.

Her visit to Arizona to visit Douglass was another turning point in Willa's life. At first she was appalled by what she found. The town was distressingly ugly, surrounded by rubbish heaps. Douglass's house was little more than a shack and his friend, Tooker, irritated her. He had gleaned most of his education from books and magazines, was in the habit of mispronouncing words, and seemed to possess an inexhaustible fund of useless information. Sometimes Willa would form sharp prejudices against people, then swiftly discard them. This was the case with Tooker. In time she was to regard him as one of her truest friends and he became the model for one of her most sympathetic portraits, that of Ray Kennedy in *The Song of the Lark.*

In spite of those two unfortunate first impressions, the trip to the Southwest became one of discovery for her. Sensitive as always to landscape, she was exhilarated by the desert with its red sand and silvery-green rabbit brush and sage. With Tooker and Douglass she began to make trips out into the desert and the upper canyons. They rode horseback and would sometimes camp out a week at a time. Perhaps it was here that her admiration for Tooker was born, for he threw off his intellectual pretensions and became a typical resourceful Westerner, one who could entertain her with a story one minute and help her down a one-hundred-fifty-foot cliff the next.

She found great joy in the Mexicans, too, with their ancient Aztec blood mixed with that of the Spanish conquerors. She made friends with them, listened to their music, and was delighted to be honored with an invitation to one of their balls. They opened for her a whole new world which she would someday use in her writing.

A Catholic priest who was a friend of her brother's invited Willa to accompany him on some of his drives to distant parishes. They talked about the country and the people, and the priest related to her the old Spanish and Indian legends that still survived.

Unlike Nebraska, where civilization was still only a few years old, this was a country with a past, and nothing brought that past home to Willa more forcefully than the cliff dwellings. She had heard about them all her life and dreamed of them in those summers of her youth down on the sandbars of the Republican River. Now Douglass took her to some ruins in Walnut Canyon. It was a tremendous emotional experience for her, standing in the cliff houses of an ancient people, finding bits of the pottery they had made and painted with their simple, beautiful designs.

Willa spent two months in the Southwest and because she was in an unusually receptive mood the impressions she formed there were perhaps more vivid than they might otherwise have been. She was free of the routine and cares of an editor's desk and perhaps knew then that she would never return to them. She allowed her mind to rest and her senses to take over, absorbing the feel of the hot sun on her skin, the sight of the red desert, the smell of the sand and the sage.

At the end of two months, she saw herself with fresh eyes. She was aware of how much she had grown as a person since she had left Red Cloud at the age of twenty-two. Those last years at *McClure's* particularly had been years of growth and she was eager to see what they meant to her as a writer.

When she left Arizona, she stopped off in Red Cloud on her return to the East. She spent June and July there. Wheat harvest was in full swing. She felt as carefree as she had when a child and found herself soaking up the scents, colors, and sounds of the prairie as she had then. Filtered through the perceptions and senses of the woman she had become, a new vision of Nebraska developed within her and struggled for expression. The result was a story about the prairie called "The White Mulberry Tree," which she wrote in Pittsburgh, again a guest of Isabelle McClung's.

This story had the same setting as "Alexandra," the story which she had not offered for publication. She combined the two, enlarged upon them, and came up with *O Pioneers!*, the novel which marked a definite change in her life. Not only were the reviews encouraging, but she felt that at last she knew the character of her talent and the direction in which it was leading her. Her editing days were over; from now on she would devote full time to her writing.

ten

Upon returning to New York from her visit to the
Southwest and Red Cloud, Willa moved into an apartment at 5 Bank Street in Greenwich Village. Edith Lewis,
a member of the *McClure's* staff who had become a good
friend of Willa's, chose the apartment. The two women
had shared a Greenwich Village apartment previously but
had given it up during Willa's long stay in the West. The
fifteen years she was to live at 5 Bank Street were to be
Willa Cather's best working years.

The apartment house was a wide brick structure of five
stories. It had been built by a wealthy brewer as a
wedding present to his son and had later been made into
an apartment house with two apartments on each floor.

The one in which Miss Lewis and Willa Cather lived was on the second floor facing the street. It possessed seven large rooms, all with high ceilings and big windows. The three front rooms were used as one large living room.

The house possessed no central heating unit. The dining room and living room each contained a fireplace with a coal grate. Small copper-lined stoves were bought to heat the two bedrooms. The house was not wired for electricity but it was lighted by gas, which sometimes froze in cold weather.

In spite of these inconveniences, Willa loved the apartment. It was to give her the first solid roots she had had since leaving Red Cloud. She took immense pleasure in furnishing it, hiring an Italian carpenter to build some low bookshelves, hanging copies of Tintorettos, Giorgiones, and Titians that she had brought from Italy. She and Miss Lewis bought mahogany chests and a round mahogany dining table for a few dollars at auction houses. Some comfortable chairs and some large Oriental rugs completed their furnishings.

The house was solidly built, with thick walls that shut out the cold in winter and the heat in summer. Very few noises from the street or their neighbors filtered through. A German family living overhead had their apartment thickly carpeted and the only sounds that came down through the ceiling were those of their daughter's piano practice in the mornings. So long as they lived there, she practiced only one thing—Beethoven's *Appassionata*—but after a while, Willa began to like this practicing. She told Miss Lewis it was like a signal to work and she came to associate it with her working hours.

Elizabeth Shepley Sergeant thus described the house and her first visit there:

"When it [the door] was opened by an exuberant maid out poured a heavy-spicy perfume of summer flowers. . . . Willa's work was carried on, at any season, within a fragile screen of hovering flower-scents and gay petals.

"Later, I was to know her apartment in winter, by the smell of orange blossoms, camellias, violets, freesias. I was to see it in spring, when jonquils and narcissus stood on the table, and lilac and dogwood branched on the mantel.

"Willa stood reticent, confident, as I gazed about me. Everything in the rooms but the flowers was simple, plain, all but Spartan. There was space, and the good windows and marble fireplace asserted their lines. In this walled stronghold of her very self, a plain desk, a small writing table with a typewriter, and a tidy sheaf of manuscript were central.

". . . I still see the bounteous gesture of Willa's arm, well-rounded, white, pouring [at dinner] a dry Burgundy she had found for me. She had also hunted through Jefferson Market for a perfect leaf lettuce. . . . Willa's dressing, mixed at the table, was compounded of light French olive oil and of the richest wine vinegar, with a dash of tarragon. She insisted on the tarragon."

Willa Cather and Edith Lewis were fortunate to find an exceptionally capable housekeeper to work for them. Her name was Josephine Bourda; she had just come over from France and spoke no English. She lived at home with her husband, a young daughter, and her father, who had operated a well-known restaurant in France.

Josephine was a splendid cook and as a result, Willa Cather was able to give a great many dinner parties. Josephine would make no attempt to speak English and so Willa and Miss Lewis were forced to speak French with her. She created a French household atmosphere about them, and Miss Lewis believed that this contributed in some measure to two of Willa Cather's later novels, *Death Comes for the Archbishop* and *Shadows on the Rock*. Josephine continued to work for them throughout those Bank Street years.

Once the apartment was made comfortable and well

managed, Willa Cather gave no thought to acquiring new or better furniture. She preferred to spend what money she had on flowers, music, and entertaining their friends.

For a number of years Willa was at home to her friends every Friday afternoon. It is in the setting at 5 Bank Street that most of those friends remember her—the spacious rooms, the glowing fireplaces, the soft chairs, and the warm colors lent by the flowers and the Oriental rugs. Conversation flowed richly and often a small group of intimate friends would stay after the other visitors had drifted away, lingering long past the dinner hour and driving Josephine, in the kitchen, to despair.

Opera was a particular source of joy to Willa in those years. It was in one of its greatest periods with names such as Scotti, Chaliapin, and Caruso frequently appearing on the programs. Among the stars was Olive Fremstad, a mezzo-soprano. Willa was much impressed with her artistry and saw her nearly every time she performed.

She got the chance to meet Madame Fremstad personally when Cameron Mackenzie asked her to do an article on the opera for *McClure's* in 1913. She was given an appointment to meet Madame Fremstad late one afternoon at the singer's apartment near Riverside Drive. Willa was to meet Edith Lewis and Isabelle McClung at the Metropolitan Opera House after the interview and a quick supper. The three of them had tickets for *Tales of Hoffmann* that evening. Willa Cather arrived just before the curtain went up; she told them that she had not been able to interview Madame Fremstad.

She had waited in the Fremstad apartment for the singer to return from an afternoon drive. When she did, she began at once to apologize for being late. It was apparent to Willa that the woman was very tired; in fact she could scarcely speak. Her voice was little more than a hoarse whisper. She was haggard and pale. "She looked forty years old!" Willa Cather told her friends. Although Madame Fremstad was willing to go through with the interview, Willa Cather urged her to rest and said she could come back another time.

The intermission between the first and second acts that night grew longer and longer and the audience became restless. At last the manager came out before the curtain to announce that the soprano had been taken ill and that Madame Olive Fremstad had consented to appear in her place. Willa and her friends could not believe it, yet when the curtain went up, there she was and her performance was faultless. Willa Cather kept exclaiming, "But it's impossible. It's impossible!"

For an ordinary person it would have been just that, but not for an artist of the magnitude of Olive Fremstad. As a child, Fremstad had been driven hard and punishingly. Through years of disciplined effort she had learned to do the "impossible."

Willa saw Madame Fremstad often after that. She frequently had tea at the Fremstad apartment, and the singer came a number of times to Bank Street for dinner. Willa Cather found in her an artist of the kind that had always fascinated her. Fremstad's talent was a combination of intelligence and fierce originality. Through tremendous effort she had used both to transform talent into art.

Fremstad had been born in Sweden and brought to America as a child. The family settled in St. Peter, Minnesota, an area very much like the Nebraska prairie where there was neither artistic stimulus nor discriminating taste. Her father was a doctor, fanatically religious and passionately interested in music. He forced his daughter to begin giving music lessons when she was twelve, and made her pay for her own music lessons out of her earnings.

Fremstad fought her way out of St. Peter and into the cultural centers of the world with no help from her family. In her early twenties, she was in Germany studying music and had just turned thirty when she began singing at the Metropolitan Opera.

Hearing her sing was a profound experience for Willa. Some who knew Fremstad thought her cold and overbearing. There was no doubt that she could be merciless with those who crossed her. To Willa none of this mattered. She had always believed that an artist should not be judged by the same standards as were ordinary people. The tremendous effort required to master an art takes a fearful toll of an artist's personality, she thought, a constant bleeding of his strength. She was beginning to know this from her own work.

Fremstad excited Willa's imagination to such an extent that a novel began to take shape in her mind. The result was *The Song of the Lark*, the story of the development of a great singer. She began the novel in the winter of 1913–14. It flowed so easily from her pen that she discovered she could write wherever she happened to be. In the spring of 1914 she went to Pittsburgh to stay with Isabelle McClung and from there made short visits to Olive Fremstad at the singer's summer place near Bridgeport, Maine.

She spent the summer in Red Cloud and there news of the outbreak of World War I reached her. She sensed that an age had come to an end and she mourned it. Thereafter she was often heard to say, "Our present is ruined—but we had a beautiful past."

She went from Nebraska to Wyoming to visit her brother Roscoe, and from there to the Southwest. She was restless, distressed by reports of the war raging in France, a country she loved passionately. She returned to Pittsburgh and Isabelle McClung and found a measure of peace in working on her novel. It went well there and she was cheered by visits with her youngest brother, Jack, who was studying at Carnegie Institute.

In fact her novel went so well during her stay at the McClungs' that she remained there through most of the winter of 1915. Then she returned to Bank Street, was at home to no one and disconnected her phone, leaving even Olive Fremstad to ring her number in vain. She was riding a tide of creative activity more powerful than anything she had known before. She believed she could go on writing indefinitely and wanted nothing else. All personal problems fell away from her when she was writing.

The book was finished in little more than a year after its start. She was dissatisfied with it in later years, disapproving its conventional structure. One of the things she admired most in Olive Fremstad was that "she rejects one hundred means of expression for every one she uses." Willa felt that she had not done this in her novel, that she had not lifted the material into the realm of art.

Yet it pleased Olive Fremstad immensely. The childhood of Thea, the heroine, had been taken largely from Willa Cather's own youth, but Thea as a singer was modeled closely on Olive Fremstad. In fact after she read the novel, Fremstad flung her arms around Willa and declared she could not tell where Thea left off and Olive began.

In the summer of 1915 Willa presented the completed manuscript to her publisher, Houghton Mifflin, and took off with Edith Lewis for a long visit to the Southwest. It turned out to be an adventurous trip, one during which her mind lay fallow, unconsciously absorbing material which she would later use in two novels.

eleven

For many years Willa Cather had wanted to visit the
Mesa Verde cliff dwellings in southwestern Colorado.
Although early Spanish explorers gave the mesa its name,
which means "green table," there is no evidence that they
discovered the large cliff dwellings hidden in many of
the canyons. Some of the houses in the lower canyons
were discovered in the 1870s, but it was not until 1888
that the major discovery was made.

On December 18th of that year, Dick Wertherill and
Charles Mason, two cowboys in search of lost cattle, came
upon Cliff Palace, a dwelling containing more than two
hundred rooms, including many kivas, the circular cere-
monial chambers of the ancient Pueblo Indians who lived
there.

The excavations and explorations that followed revealed hundreds of prehistoric village ruins among the canyons. The most striking of these are the many-storied apartments built under overhanging cliffs.

Excavation also revealed that the Pueblo Indians had not always lived above the ground. In the seventh and eighth centuries A.D., they lived in lodges below the ground and it was not until the ninth century that they began building their adobe and stone pueblos on the surface. Then suddenly in the thirteenth century, they abandoned these for some unknown reason.

The whole story of the Mesa Verde and the mystery of the people who lived there had stirred Willa Cather's imagination for years and in the summer of 1915 she and Edith Lewis went there by train. Their point of destination was Mancos, a town twenty miles east of the Mesa Verde National Park. The road from Mancos to the park was too rough and primitive for an automobile, so the two women hired a horse-drawn wagon and a driver to take them there.

Before they left, however, Willa paid a visit to Dick Wertherill's brother, who still lived in Mancos. From him she heard first hand the story of how Dick swam the Mancos River on his horse and rode into the mesa looking for stray cattle, and of how he had come upon the cliff dwellings that had been hidden for centuries.

The Mesa Verde National Park had been created nine years before Willa's first visit. She and Edith Lewis stayed in the tourist camp the Government had set up. Since there were few guests there at the time, the forest ranger and guide, a young man named Jeep, was able to spend a great deal of his time taking the two women around to the different cliff dwellings. They spent a week there, devoting an entire day to the Cliff Palace and its tower, cooking their lunch there and drinking from the spring behind the cliff houses.

Jeep had planned a trip to the Tower House for their last day in the park, but just as they were about to start, a large group of tourists arrived and he had to see to them. He assigned his brother-in-law, a young man named Ricknor, to guide Willa and her companion. The women would have preferred not to trust themselves to a guide they knew nothing about, but since Jeep had announced the change of plan in Ricknor's presence, the women did not want to object. So they started off.

The trail by which Ricknor took them to Tower House was extremely rough. In climbing down the side of Soda Canyon they were forced in many instances to hang from a tree or rock and then drop several feet to the next rock. They could not have climbed back up this trail on their return to camp without using ropes. Ricknor therefore assured them that he would take them back by another trail, farther down the canyon.

After they had visited Tower House and it was time to start home, he could not find the trail he was looking for. Finally he admitted he did not know how they were going to get back. By then they had been tramping for several miles and had reached a place where Cliff Canyon joined Soda Canyon at right angles. Ricknor thought, but was not sure, that there was an archaeologist's camp about four miles up Cliff Canyon. He knew Dr. Jesse W. Fewkes, the archaeologist in charge, and he suggested that they hunt for this camp.

Willa, who had had enough of aimless tramping and had no assurance that they could find the camp even if they looked, said that she and Edith would remain at the intersection of the two canyons while he went on ahead to determine whether the camp was really there.

One might think that Willa would have been out of patience with the entire situation by then, but she was not. Edith Lewis, in her account of that experience, declared that the four or five hours they spent waiting for their guide to return were the most rewarding of the whole Mesa Verde trip. They settled themselves on a large flat rock at the mouth of Cliff Canyon and watched silently as the summer twilight came on and a full moon rose over the rim of the canyon. They were tired and thirsty but at peace and unworried, confident that they would eventually be found.

The canyon was particularly beautiful in the moonlight and they were enjoying the sight when they heard shouts from Cliff Canyon. A few minutes later two men appeared, members of Doctor Fewkes's party. Ricknor, who had been too exhausted to make the return trip, had sent them after the two women.

The trail back to the Fewkes camp was a mass of broken rocks, some of them as big as houses. Without the aid and comfort of their cheerful guides, the women would never have made it. At one place Willa and Edith had to lie down and be pulled through a sort of tunnel of rocks.

They reached the Fewkes camp at about two in the morning. The two archaeologists immediately rounded up two of their horses, hitched them to a wagon, and drove Ricknor and the two women back to their own camp.

Edith Lewis said that on the whole they enjoyed this adventure. They were tired and stiff for a day or two afterward, but otherwise they suffered no ill effects from it.

This was Willa's only visit to the Mesa Verde. For eight years her impressions of it lay at the back of her mind. It was not until 1923 that the mysterious chemistry of imagination and impression produced the novel *The Professor's House.*

From the Mesa Verde Willa and Edith went to Taos, New Mexico. It was a difficult place to get to at that time. They had to drive a long way by team over a rough road and when they arrived, they found no American hotel or boardinghouse. They stayed in a primitive adobe hotel run by a Mexican woman.

They spent a month there exploring the country on horseback or with a team they drove themselves. It was an excellent way to see the country, much better than driving along a superhighway. They could go wherever they wished, but it was necessary to note every landmark so they would not lose their way.

The following summer Willa and Edith again visited Taos. Willa was not consciously gathering material for a book or a story. She had no thought at the time of writing about anything she was seeing or feeling. She went to the Southwest because she loved it passionately. She found in the Southwest a country that excited her as the Nebraska prairie always had. The Mexicans, too, interested her in the same way the Scandinavian and Bohemian settlers on the prairie had.

During one of those summers in Taos she drove a team to Arroyo Hondo, and Edith Lewis noted her excitement over the place and the dramatic approach to it. Years afterward the memory became part of *Death Comes for the Archbishop*.

Another time a hailstorm overtook the two women as they were riding horseback through the desert and forced them to take cover in a Mexican hut. Willa's impression of the hut and the Mexican woman who lived there also became a part of *Death Comes for the Archbishop*. Slight incidents such as these could lie in her mind for years and be brought to life again in her writing.

The book that took shape in her imagination after those two summers in the Southwest had nothing to do with that country, however. It was the result of a visit she made during a stopover in Red Cloud at the end of one of those summers. The book, *My Ántonia*, was to be written about the Nebraska prairie and one woman who spent her life there. It would place Willa Cather solidly in the ranks of America's great artists.

twelve

In the spring of 1916 Willa was in New York and went to have tea in the apartment of her friend Elizabeth Shepley Sergeant. Since Miss Sergeant's apartment was near Central Park, where Willa often walked, she went on foot and arrived there, with her cheeks reddened from the winter crispness that remained in the air. Miss Sergeant remarked once that she thought of Willa Cather as always wearing red-brown fur in winter in those years. It made her hair shine.

While the teakettle boiled, they talked of Henry James. Willa Cather had been a great admirer of his and had imitated his style in some of her early writing. In his *Notes on Novelists* he had stated a truth that Willa had not forgotten. The book lay on Miss Sergeant's writing table and Willa turned to the passage. In it James declares that a reporter must write one way, a creative writer another, and that the two methods cannot be combined harmoniously.

Willa Cather observed that she had not completely banished the reporter-like style from her last book. Henceforth she would aim at a form and technique that would be simpler. Her object would be to leave out everything she could and still achieve the effect she wanted.

Leaning over then, she set an old Sicilian apothecary jar filled with orange-brown flowers of scented stock in the middle of a round, antique table that was otherwise bare. She said that she wanted her new heroine to be like that—"like a rare object in the middle of a table, which one may examine from all sides."

Saying this, she moved a lamp so that the light streamed brightly down on the jar with its glazed orange and blue design. "I want her to stand out like this—" her voice faltered under the force of some sudden emotion and her eyes filled with tears "—like this because she *is* the story."

"Was it someone you knew in your childhood?" Miss Sergeant asked.

Willa Cather nodded but did not say more.

Miss Sergeant was never sure whether Willa Cather had been thinking of Ántonia or Mrs. Forrester, the heroine of *A Lost Lady*, for she often thought about her heroines for years before she put them in her writing. It was when *My Ántonia* was published two years later that Miss Sergeant recalled the scene.

At the end of each of her summer visits to the Southwest in 1915 and 1916, Willa Cather stopped off in Red Cloud on her return to New York. It was in 1916 during her stay in Nebraska that she drove out to the Divide to visit an old friend, Anna Pavelka.

"One of the people who interested me most as a child," Willa wrote several years later, "was the Bohemian hired girl of one of our neighbors who was so good to me. She was one of the truest artists I ever knew in the keenness and sensitiveness of her enjoyment, in her love of people, and in her willingness to take pains. I did not realize all this as a child, but Annie fascinated me and I always had it in mind to write a story about her."

Willa Cather always criticized people who thought that art was something separate, something to be tacked onto life. She believed that artistic appreciation should include all the activities of life. She once said that "the German housewife who sets before her family on Thanksgiving Day a perfectly roasted goose is an artist. The farmer who goes out in the morning to harness his team and pauses to admire the sunrise—he is an artist." In Anna Pavelka, Willa Cather found such a person.

Annie had come to America with her parents and brothers and sisters when she was twelve. Her father was one of those who were not strong enough to fight the prairie and committed suicide. Annie helped take over the farm and did a man's work, plowing the tough prairie sod, planting and harvesting, and trying to keep the family from starving.

When her brothers were old enough to handle the farm themselves, she sought work in town as a hired girl. The Miners hired her to do kitchen chores and housework, although she had never had time to learn to cook and to sew. She learned quickly and when Mrs. Miner gave her permission to use the sewing machine, she made all the shirts and overalls and husking gloves for her own family. She made everyday shoes for herself, cutting insoles from cardboard and covering them with several layers of oil-cloth. The tops she made from wool or denim. These awkward devices, tied to her feet with black tape, flapped as she moved but did not slow her down as she scurried about her tasks.

The Miner children took Annie with them to the Opera House shows, but above all else Annie liked to dance. No matter how hard she worked during the day, she would dance all night if she had the chance. For her dancing she needed better shoes than those she made and better dresses too. All of Annie's wages were to go to her family since she was under eighteen, but Carrie Miner saw to it that Annie kept enough money to buy shoes when she needed them. Much to the annoyance of many girls around town, Annie learned to copy any dress that caught her eye.

Annie left Red Cloud to marry a brakeman on the Burlington Railroad, but her husband deserted her after only a few weeks, and she returned to Webster County and her mother's dugout.

During the years Willa Cather was attending college and starting to work in the East, she lost track of Anna Pavelka. When they met again, Annie was the wife of a Bohemian farmer on the Divide and the mother of a large family that captivated Willa. The daughters were beautiful and the sons were champions in the county weight-lifting and boxing contests and star athletes on the high-school basketball and football teams.

Willa had always been sensitive to weather and when she made her visits to Annie's home, she carried an assortment of wraps and scarves. When Annie's boys took her to her carriage at their farm gate, each had a wrap over his arm. They would help her into her carriage with a flourish and tuck the wraps about her. Returning home exhausted from the excitement of her visit, she would exclaim, "The manners of Annie's sons would do credit to the family of a grand duke!"

Annie's husband was as proud of their children as his

wife was. When neighbors advised him to sell his cream and buy more land with the money he made from it, he agreed with Annie that roses in the cheeks of their children were more important than land or money in the bank.

One of Annie's sons said of her, "She was happier with a crust of bread and a new baby than someone else would be with a million dollars. I never saw her unhappy."

When Willa saw Anna Pavelka that summer of 1916, worn with work but fulfilled and still brimming with life, surrounded by her husband and their large brood of happy children, the impression struck fire in her imagination. To her this Bohemian woman was a symbol of triumph. She had not been squeezed dry by the prairie or by the narrowness of the community in which she lived. She had not had to escape to the East in order to remain herself as Willa had had to do. By the time Willa returned to New York, she had already completed the first two or three chapters of *My Ántonia*.

During the winter and the following spring, she worked steadily on her new book. Early in the summer of 1917, she joined Isabelle McClung in Jaffrey, New Hampshire. Isabelle had married that past year. Her husband was Jan Hambourg, the violinist who had often visited the McClung home in Pittsburgh while Willa Cather lived there.

The marriage had been something of a blow to Willa. Since she had no husband and children of her own, her friendships were tremendously important to her, Isabelle's most of all. Isabelle had always protected her, having provided a quiet place for her to write during her Pittsburgh days. And even after Willa Cather had established a home in New York, she spent several months each year in the McClung home in Pittsburgh. Isabelle had inspired her in her work as no one else had been able to do. She had been an animating force in Willa's life, and her marriage brought to Willa a sharp sense of loss. Not only could their friendship never again be quite the same, but Willa was afraid that once the war ended, the Hambourgs would make their home in Europe.

She accepted Isabelle's invitation to join her and Jan at the Shattuck Inn in Jaffrey. The visit had happy results. Although Willa had spent some months in Boston during her *McClure* days, she had never gotten beyond the edge of New England. She discovered the region now and found it enchanting. Jaffrey became one of the best places for her to work, a replacement for the refuge in the McClung home that she had lost.

She took two small rooms on the top floor of the Shattuck Inn. They had sloping ceilings, like her attic room at home in Red Cloud, and the windows looked out over woods and juniper pastures to Mount Monadnock in the background. Whenever she returned to Jaffrey, she rented these same two rooms.

The room next to hers was occupied by a bellboy who had been warned by the managers that he must be very quiet so he would not disturb Miss Cather.

The Shattuck Inn was crowded that summer and to give her the solitude and quiet she needed to write, two more of her Pittsburgh friends, Miss Lucy Hine and Miss Acheson, who rented a place not far from the inn, put up a tent in their meadow for Willa to work in. This arrangemen proved to be an excellent one. The tent, furnished with a table and camp chair, stood about half a mile from the inn. To get to it Willa had to walk through the woods and across several fields. She loved these walks and found them the best possible preparation for a morning's work. She wrote for two or three hours every day. In the afternoons she would take long walks about the countryside and up the mountain, generally carrying Mathews' *Field*

Book of American Flowers, her favorite branch of botany. Her love of flowers went back to the days of her childhood on the prairie, when her one consolation in all that bleakness was the wild flowers she found growing there. She used to gather them in heaps and weep over them because no one else seemed to notice them.

Willa returned to Jaffrey the next year. By then *My Ántonia* had been completed and turned over to her publisher. The proofs were ready by the time she and Edith Lewis arrived at the Shattuck Inn and they spent those first few weeks going over them. Reading proofs is a boring task and Willa liked to read them out of doors whenever possible. She and Edith carried them into the woods each morning and, leaning back against a convenient rock or tree trunk, Willa made corrections while chipmunks flashed up and down nearby trees.

Unlike many writers, Willa did not mind striking out words or passages once she had written them. If she believed a book would be improved by cutting them out, she did not hesitate to do so. Her corrections on the proofs of *My Ántonia* were so numerous that she had to pay the publisher nearly $150 to make the changes. Afterward, she was more careful, making most of her corrections in the typewritten copies of her manuscripts.

Houghton Mifflin published the book that fall (1918). It was very different from books that had been published up to that time, so different in fact as to be revolutionary. The criticism that it was not precisely a novel always made Willa impatient. Of course it wasn't! She had not intended it should be and had made that plain in the preface. In the book she had gathered memories of persons and places very dear to her. Everything in the book was there to establish a feeling, not to tell a story.

Story or not, the material holds the reader. He is constantly required to make comparisons between the two groups who settled the prairie: the immigrant families and the families from the Eastern states. In every instance the reader is led to see the superiority of the immigrant families, who had been shaped by their Old World culture, over those of American stock, who demanded a rigid conformity, a sameness, from everyone.

Then there is the glowing portrait of Ántonia herself— as a girl and later as a woman. Willa's admiration for her was boundless. She had once remarked to Elizabeth Shepley Sergeant that nothing could be more beautiful, if you had it in you, than to be the wife of a farmer and raise a big family in Nebraska. Willa Cather had chosen the lonely life of a writer and had no regrets, yet she could look at a woman like Anna Pavelka, her Ántonia, and feel that this was how one should have lived if one could.

She never lost touch with Anna Pavelka again, visiting her and her family whenever she returned to Red Cloud, or writing letters and sending gifts. She once sent a check for fifty dollars to Annie, telling her to buy herself a present, but taxes on the farm were due and Annie paid them off instead, never revealing to her friend what the gift money had paid for. Willa was aware that the family was often short of money although they would never ask for help; she kept informed of their situation through mutual friends. She wrote one of those friends asking if Annie's oldest son was planting hybrid corn. If he was not, Willa meant to see that he could afford to do so the next year. During the severe drought in the 1930's she sent money each year so that they could buy seed wheat.

Believing that *My Ántonia* was the best thing she had ever done, Willa was disappointed in Houghton Mifflin's treatment of it. They did not seem to share her enthusiasm for the book and did not push its sales as she believed they should have. In the first year *My Ántonia* brought

Willa Cather only thirteen hundred dollars and not quite four hundred dollars the second year. She began to feel that she could never write a book that would be completely satisfactory to this publishing house and so she began to look for another.

Her search took her to a New York publisher who had been in business only a few years but whose standards of excellence impressed Willa. Alfred A. Knopf was a young man who seemed to be trying to do something unusual and individual in publishing. The attractive books he was bringing out contrasted sharply with the rather plain covers Houghton Mifflin had given Willa's books.

She went to Knopf's office for the first time in the early spring of 1920 to size him up. What she saw and heard impressed her. While they talked about books, those they liked and those they disliked, she noticed some samples of blue binding paper lying on his desk. He told her he intended to use the binding paper for a book of Chinese poems he was publishing. He had gone to the Metropolitan Museum of Art to find exactly the right shade of blue from among the Chinese porcelains and paintings. It was this meticulous concern for detail that won her over. Before leaving his office, she asked Mr. Knopf to be her publisher. He suggested they think longer about the matter since changing publishers was a serious business.

At their second meeting a few days later, Mr. Knopf agreed to become her publisher and asked if she had anything ready to publish. She was at work on a novel and had nothing to offer him but a collection of short stories. Five of them had appeared previously in magazines; the rest she had written since completing *My Ántonia*. A few months later Mr. Knopf put them out in a volume entitled *Youth and the Bright Medusa*.

Edith Lewis believed that Willa's choice of Alfred Knopf as her publisher influenced her career more than anything she had ever done. Her books began earning her a great deal of money, and the financial security that resulted lifted a great burden from Willa's shoulders. She had never been able to get used to the fact that she was no longer earning a salary.

Her relationship with Mr. Knopf brought her another, and perhaps even more important, kind of security, for he never ceased encouraging her to write exactly as she felt she should. He made evident not only to her but to the whole world his great admiration for and belief in her. Willa no longer felt that she must defend herself against the doubters and those persons who wished to belittle her work. Although she was always modest about her work, she had great pride. Now with the strength of Alfred Knopf's approval behind her, her pride was no longer threatened.

thirteen

The novel that Willa was at work on when she first visited Alfred Knopf was *One of Ours*. It was the story of a boy of exceptional sensitivity who was undergoing a slow strangulation of intellect and feeling on the Nebraska prairie where he had been born. His induction into the army at the outbreak of World War I provided an escape and an unexpected opportunity for the growth of his character and personality.

The war touched Willa deeply. She loved France and could not bear to think of the French countryside's being torn and laid waste by the battles being waged there. It touched her in other ways too. A steady stream of soldiers from Lincoln, Red Cloud, and Pittsburgh, boys she knew or who were friends of friends, stopped by her New York apartment to visit her. Many of them were on their last furloughs before being sent overseas.

Yet the idea for a novel about the war did not occur to her until news arrived, in May, 1918, of the death in battle of a young cousin of hers, George P. Cather, Jr. He had grown up in Webster County along with Willa Cather and her brothers and sisters. Later he had served in the Navy and the National Guard. He had become so extraordinarily skillful with big guns that when he enlisted in the Army at the beginning of World War I, he was made a lieutenant almost immediately. He was killed in the Battle of Cantigny, the first American offensive in France.

His mother allowed Willa to read some of the letters he had written home and she was amazed at how his military experience had changed him. He had grown and developed more as a person during his short term in the Army than in all the years he had spent on the Nebraska prairie. What had brought about this change?

She observed the same astonishing change in another young man whose acquaintance she had made. She did not know him well; in fact she had met him only three times. He was David Hockstein, a talented violinist. Willa first met him in the winter of 1916, when he played in a quintet at an informal musical party at a New York hotel. She found her affection and her imagination captured by him from the start. He was about twenty-four, reserved, refreshingly sincere, and had talent, which she respected as she did all real talent.

She did not meet him again until the following year. By then the United States had entered the war, and David Hockstein was torn between his loyalty to the United States and his affection for Germany. He had studied for a time there and was a great admirer of German culture. Moreover, he did not believe in those slogans that everyone else was trumpeting—that this was the "war to end all wars," or that this one would "make the world safe for democracy." He did not believe the war was going to accomplish anything good, no matter how it came out.

Many of his fellow artists believed he should be exempt from military duty. He himself hated the idea of giving up his work and going into the Army, yet he was repelled by the idea of being a shirker. Nevertheless, he appealed for an exemption shortly thereafter. When the local draft board discovered that he was the sole support of his mother, they granted him a deferment. This did not satisfy him for long and he eventually went to his board, told them he had made arrangements for his mother, and now wished to enter the Army.

A few weeks after his induction Willa saw him again and found him deeply depressed. The discipline, the deadening dullness of the constant drilling, the boredom, and the frustrating feeling that he was wasting time were very hard for him to bear. He missed the companionship of his fellow artists. He had found no one in the Army with whom he had anything in common. He told Willa that his mind felt heavy, as if it had been drugged. She noticed that he looked older and that his face was full of bitter resignation.

Three months later she saw him for the last time and was struck by the change in him. His expression was now alert and confident, and a glow of enthusiasm came into his eyes when he talked about his life in the Army. When questioned about the change, he had some difficulty explaining it, but he declared he was no longer bored and the men he lived and worked with were splendid. He said, "For me there is something in that life . . . something I've always wanted."

In the autumn of 1918 he was killed in the Battle of the Argonne. As in the case of her cousin, Willa was given some of the dead man's letters to read. They brought the same questions to her mind that her cousin's letters had: How had they changed so much and so quickly, this sensitive and talented boy from New York and the Nebraska farm boy with his scant education and experience in life? What was there about the Army and the war in France that had brought about a similar effect in two dissimilar boys? Willa Cather's search for these answers led to the writing of *One of Ours*.

The book took shape slowly. She began it late in 1918 and was still working on it the next fall when she went to Jaffrey, New Hampshire, for a few months' stay. Writing steadily in her tent in the meadow despite the fact that the season was unusually damp and rainy, she fell ill with influenza. The local doctor who was called upon to treat her had had a great deal of experience with that disease. He had been medical officer on a troopship during the war when an epidemic of flu broke out. He not only brought Willa through her illness, but he offered her the diary he had kept during the war. It proved a rich mine and provided much of the material for the fourth part of *One of Ours*. After the book was published the doctor related an amusing incident to her. He had been telling an acquaintance about an experience he had had during the war, and the acquaintance said indignantly, "That's not a true story. You took it from Willa Cather's book."

By the spring of 1920 she was two thirds of her way through the novel. The remainder of the action would take place in France, and Willa felt that she must live in that country for a while before she could write more. In June she and Edith Lewis went by ocean liner to France and took rooms in a Paris hotel that looked out upon the Seine. Friends had given Willa letters of introduction to important people, but she did not use them. Outside of an occasional visit to the opera, she remained for the most part on the Left Bank of the Seine, trying to turn her vision backward to the Paris of the Middle Ages. This medieval period had nothing to do with her novel, but she felt she must return that far into the past in order to grasp French civilization as a whole. She was successful because of her extraordinary knack of sensing the essence of a particular historical period. Some of the impressions she accumulated of the old Paris she was to use years later in another novel, *Shadows on the Rock*.

At the end of seven weeks Isabelle and Jan Hambourg arrived in Paris and took Willa Cather on a two-week tour of the battlefields and the scarred countryside. She found her cousin's grave and wrote a long letter to his mother about it.

Once this tour was completed, she felt that she had all the material necessary to finish the book and was eager to return home and resume writing. Despite her eagerness, however, the last third of the book went slowly too, and it was September, 1922, before it was at last published. It had taken her four years to write it.

One of Ours, like *The Song of the Lark*, illustrates the development of an exceptional individual. In *The Song of the Lark* Thea Kronborg possesses a great talent and the strength of will to develop it regardless of the obstacles she has to overcome. Claude Wheeler, the main character in *One of Ours*, possesses neither. His exceptional quality is his extreme sensitivity, which is being strangled in the early part of the book by the people and atmosphere which prevail in the small prairie town where he lives.

These repressive factors are symbolized by Claude's brother, Bayliss, whose main goal in life is to make money. He considers everything else unimportant. Surrounded by people like his brother, Claude begins to doubt the value of his own taste and judgment, to wonder if he is wrong and queer because he believes there are things in life more important than making money.

When he enters the Army and goes to France, he finds that he is not mistaken or odd. There *are* other values in the world besides those of his narrow, mindless hometown. Now he is free to grow and he does so. Near the end of the book he reflects that no battlefield or shattered country he had seen is as ugly as this world would be if men like his brother controlled it altogether.

In writing this book Willa was saying that the splendid pioneer period was over. No longer could one remain on the prairie and fulfill oneself as Ántonia had done. Now one had to go away from the prairie to grow. All that had encouraged Willa Cather's own growth was dead or dying because of the rigid demands of the community to conform. There were no more individuals like William Ducker, Mrs. Charles Wiener, or Professor Shindelmeisser. The people were all as much alike as if they had been cut by the same cookie cutter and that was the way they wanted to be. They resented anyone who tried to introduce a new idea or a different way of looking at things. They were self-satisfied and proud in their ignorance and mediocrity.

One of Ours won for Willa Cather the Pulitzer prize. She was always to say that, among all the characters she created in her fiction, Claude Wheeler was her favorite.

fourteen

By the time Willa Cather received word of her Pulitzer prize in May, 1923, she had completed her next novel, *A Lost Lady*. A change had been taking place in her and it could be seen in the downward movement of this book. It did not end on a high point—success or self-fulfillment —as her other novels had done. Instead it told of the decline of a woman and a village.

Willa did not like the direction American life was taking. She saw this most sharply in Nebraska, where democracy was growing more and more to mean dullness and sameness. The Bohemian farm wife's recipe for roast goose, handed down for generations, was no longer treasured. She was encouraged to create her meals from tin cans. Her children were thought queer because they spoke a foreign tongue. When they started to school, they were taught that English was the only proper language to speak.

Willa despised the machine and believed mechanization was the worst thing that could have happened to America. "We have music by machines, we travel by machines—the American people are so submerged in them that sometimes I think they can only be made to laugh and cry by machinery."

She believed the machine might in the end kill American art and in an interview in New York she told why. "The Frenchman," she said, "doesn't talk nonsense about art, about self-expression; he is too greatly occupied with building the things that make his home. His house, his garden, his vineyards, these are the things that fill his mind. He creates something beautiful, something lasting. And what happens? When a French painter wants to paint a picture, he makes a copy of a garden, a home, a village. The art in them inspires his brush. And twenty, thirty, forty years later you will come to see the original of that picture and you'll find it changed only by the mellowness of time.

"Restlessness such as ours, success such as ours do not make for beauty. Other things must come first; good cookery, cottages that are homes, not playthings; gardens, repose. These are first-rate things, and out of first-rate stuff art is made. It is possible that machinery has finished us as far as this is concerned. Nobody stays at home anymore; nobody makes anything beautiful anymore."

Friends, aware of her pessimism, and critics noted a remark she made in a prefatory note to *Not Under Forty:* "The world broke in two in 1922 or thereabout, and I belonged to the former half." The war seemed to have changed everything. All the old, solid values in American life were being discarded as it rushed toward a future that Willa Cather believed would be mechanized and ugly. It was the past she admired and found so beautiful that she had written some of her finest books and short stories about it.

In *A Lost Lady* she showed how the strength and vigor of the pioneer period gave way to a mean, moneygrubbing era. The "lost lady" of the novel was based on a woman whom Willa had known during her childhood in Red Cloud—Mrs. Silas Garber. Her husband, while a captain in the Union Army, had heard from a Mexican in his outfit about the unbelievably fertile Republican River Valley, where grass grew as high as a man's head. In the spring of 1870, he and his two brothers explored the valley on horseback. Silas Garber staked a homestead claim where Red Cloud now stands. Three years later he was elected governor of Nebraska.

Shortly after his election, he went to California to visit his brother and brought back a bride, pretty, gay, and years younger than he. She proved to be one of the most beautiful and charming hostesses ever to grace the governor's mansion. When the governor's term ended, they returned to Red Cloud to live. Willa was a frequent guest at the many parties Mrs. Garber gave, and often went driving with the governor's wife and her friends.

Ill health and the loss of his fortune clouded the governor's mind. Mrs. Garber gave even more parties, hoping the young people she invited would stimulate him and rouse him mentally. For this she was criticized and gossiped about.

After the governor's death, she lost the remainder of his money. Eventually she returned to California and married another prominent man. This provoked even more gossip, but her friends remained loyal to her. Willa had loved and admired this beautiful, vivacious woman, and the memory of her at last became a book which was considered by many critics to be the most nearly perfect in form of all her novels.

Willa Cather had more trouble with *A Lost Lady* than with any of her other books. As a rule she did not have to search for the best way to tell a story. She simply sat down and began to write and found that the best way came naturally to her. But Mrs. Forrester, the heroine of the book, was drawn so directly from Mrs. Silas Garber that Willa Cather found herself facing a serious problem. Although both Mr. and Mrs. Garber were dead, some of their relatives were alive and might be offended.

In an attempt to overcome this problem, she at first set the story in Colorado rather than Nebraska. After much writing, she realized this would not work. Her memories of Mrs. Garber and the Garber house were among the strongest impressions of her childhood. She could not transfer them to a strange place. So she began the book again, writing of things just as she remembered them, but she did not like the shape this gave the story. She continued to experiment until she hit upon the proper method for telling it. It was not to be a long, detailed novel like *One of Ours* and *The Song of the Lark.* Instead it was short, the story being told in a series of images.

It was while she was working on *A Lost Lady* that Willa Cather discovered a new place to live and write. This was Grand Manan, an island lying off the northernmost coast of Maine. It lies at the mouth of the Bay of Fundy and belongs to Canada. For their first few summers there, Edith Lewis and Willa rented a cottage, but three years later, in 1925, they had one of their own built. Living conditions were rather primitive. Mail and most supplies were brought from the mainland by boat, a trip of five or six hours. This steamboat made the trip only twice a week from St. John, New Brunswick.

Yet the beauty of the place and the pleasant climate made up for the inconveniences. The days were warm and bright and the nights cool. It rained often, but rainy weather there was not dull or gloomy. Willa found it lovely, even fascinating. Most of the island was covered with trees. On three sides the land broke off in high cliffs as it met the sea, but along one side, the land fell in a gradual slope toward the water. There four or five fishing villages had grown up, with herring fishing the chief industry.

Willa was greatly taken with the place from the first and decided it would make an ideal summer camp for her. Once she had her own cottage, it would offer a place where she would not have to make reservations or prior arrangements. She could come and go as she liked.

After completing *A Lost Lady*, Willa went to France for a stay with Jan and Isabelle Hambourg. It was while she was there that she asked Léon Bakst to paint her portrait. Nebraska had finally awakened to the fact that it had produced a famous writer, and the Omaha Society of Fine Arts had raised money for a portrait to be hung in the Omaha Public Library.

Willa Cather chose Bakst on the advice of friends although he was not a portrait painter. He was well known for his painting of background scenery for theaters and even better known for the role he played in the development of the Russian ballet.

The portrait required twenty sittings; Willa enjoyed them all. She was delighted with Bakst himself and the talks she had with him and his friends. During one sitting, the great Russian dancer, Nijinsky, was introduced to her.

After several sittings Willa realized the portrait was going to be a failure. It was dark and lifeless. Bakst realized the truth too, but nothing he tried would bring the portrait to life. Willa said nothing. It had been her mistake, asking him to attempt a work that was not in his line. Besides she knew that he was supporting a number of Russian refugees and was in great need of money.

No word of criticism came from the people of Omaha when the portrait was finally hung in the public library and Willa Cather was always grateful to them for their tact and kindness.

fifteen

Between the fall of 1923 and the summer of 1925, Willa Cather produced two more novels, *The Professor's House* and *My Mortal Enemy*. It was during a trip to the Southwest in the summer of 1925 that the idea for *Death Comes for the Archbishop* came to her. From the time of her first trip to France—perhaps even before—she had been an admirer of French culture. Over the years the compulsion grew within her to write about how the French had brought their culture to the New World and left their mark.

In the course of a hot and sleepless night in Santa Fe that summer of 1925, she came by chance upon a book called *The Life of the Right Reverend Joseph P.*

Machebeuf by Father W. J. Howlett. It had been published privately in Pueblo, Colorado, in 1908, and it is
doubtful that Willa had ever heard of it. Once she started
it, she could not put it down. She read through most of
the night.

The book told the story of two French missionary
priests who had been sent to the American Southwest in
1852 to re-establish the authority of the Roman Catholic
Church. The Catholic faith had been brought to the
region by Spanish explorers centuries earlier, but the
American church had been out of touch with Rome for so
long that it had changed. Some of the priests had even
married and were raising families.

Willa saw in the struggle by the French to tame this
wild land a similarity with the struggle the Nebraska
pioneers had waged to subdue the prairie. She also saw
that by retelling the story of the two French priests, she
could express all the love she felt for this desert country
and re-create for the reader all of the beauty that she
found in it.

In one furious blaze of creativity the book she wanted
to write took shape in her mind. By morning she saw it
whole. From that point on she knew exactly what material
she would need to write this story and she drew it out of
everything and everyone she encountered—taxi drivers,
Indians, priests, trainmen, old settlers, old books which
she brought home by the armful from the Santa Fe
library, and from the country itself, which she and Edith
Lewis toured by automobile. Willa occasionally made
notes of dates and facts that she took from her reading
but made no notes about the things she saw or was told
by the people to whom she talked. She knew that her
memory would retain whatever was of real interest or
importance.

When she left the Southwest that fall, she went straight

to Jaffrey, New Hampshire, and wrote the introduction to *Death Comes for the Archbishop*. Returning then to 5 Bank Street, she worked all winter on the book with, as Edith Lewis said, "unusual happiness and serenity." They made another trip to New Mexico in July to enable Willa to check numerous details and facts and visit some more of the places that she would be writing about in her book.

Death Comes for the Archbishop was published in the fall of 1927. It was an instant success and caught the publishers unprepared. It was so different from what was being done by other writers of that period that there was some doubt about how the public would receive it. In point of fact the demand for the book was so great that booksellers ran out of stock, and the publisher had to run off another printing.

Although Willa Cather believed that *My Ántonia* was the best thing she had ever done and that with it she had made a contribution to American letters, many critics judged *Death Comes for the Archbishop* her greatest artistic triumph. In 1930, when Sinclair Lewis was awarded the Nobel Prize for literature, he declared that it should have gone to Willa Cather.

During the year in which *Death Comes for the Archbishop* was published, a series of changes and dislocations in Willa Cather's life began. That fall she and Edith Lewis had to move out of their apartment at 5 Bank Street to allow the building to be torn down. Leaving there was a wrenching experience for Willa emotionally and physically. It was the first real home she had had after leaving Red Cloud. The years in between had been filled with a succession of dreary boardinghouse rooms, except for those months she had lived in the McClung home in Pittsburgh. Edith Lewis believed that Willa did her happiest writing in the fifteen years she lived at 5 Bank

Street—works ranging from *O Pioneers!* to *Death Comes for the Archbishop.*

"Although parts of them were written in other places, chiefly Jaffrey and Grand Manan," Miss Lewis wrote, "they all came back to Bank Street. It was there they had their home. Those years from 1912 to 1927 were for her years of absorbing and delightful experiment and discovery. All the time she was steadily developing her powers as an artist and I think the consciousness of this gave her the deepest contentment."

Willa Cather and Edith Lewis took rooms at the Grosvenor Hotel, a few steps from Washington Square and not far from their old address at 5 Bank Street. The rooms were cramped and sunless and not at all satisfactory, but it was meant to be only a temporary arrangement until they could decide what to do. As it turned out, they stayed five years at the Grosvenor, for ill health hit the families of both women and kept them traveling so much during those years that they did not have time to seek a new home.

Only a few months after Willa was forced to leave the apartment at 5 Bank Street, her father fell ill. It was while she was spending Christmas in Red Cloud that Charles Cather suffered his first heart attack. Shortly after her return to New York in March, 1928, he died. She returned at once to Red Cloud.

At first she could not accept the fact of his death. Always strong-willed, hating change of any kind, she was furious with Life for taking her father from her. She paced back and forth between the house and the Episcopal church where his body lay, wringing her hands in a frenzy of grief and frustration. Her old friends talked with her for hours before they managed to calm her.

After the funeral Willa's mother was exhausted from her sorrow and from the weeks she had spent nursing her husband. Douglass Cather, who was then living in California, persuaded his mother to accompany him when he returned to his home. This break-up of what Willa Cather had never ceased to consider home proved to be permanent. She had probably foreseen this when her father died. Perhaps that was another reason for her violent rebellion against the fact of his death. Strong-willed as she was, Time and Death were stronger.

But she fought against them. Her parents' home was the emotional center of her life. The thought of losing it sent her into a panic and made her determined to keep it going. Not long after her mother went to California, Willa decided to redecorate the house and make it ready for her mother's return.

This was not the house Willa had grown up in—the crowded, ill-designed house with her attic room. Charles Cather had bought a different house after Willa went to Pittsburgh. This one was large, well-arranged, and located in a better part of town. Because her parents had lived there and because she had visited them every year for several months at a time, it had become home to her and now with great enthusiasm she set about choosing new wallpaper and draperies. The parlor she left as it was, aware that it was her mother's favorite room. That her mother was destined never to return, Willa did not know then.

When she and Edith Lewis went to Grand Manan that summer, they decided to go by a roundabout way, through Quebec, in order to see some new country. Quebec took Willa by surprise. She knew, of course, of its French origin, but she had not believed it could keep its French character, separated from France as it was by centuries and an ocean. But when she looked down upon it from her hotel window, she saw a town so much like those she had seen in her beloved France, her interest was caught immediately.

Edith fell ill with influenza on the night of their arrival and was forced to remain in bed. During the ten days they spent in Quebec, Willa walked alone about the city, absorbing its character. It happened that their hotel possessed an excellent library of Canadian history and Willa read hungrily.

By the time they left Quebec, Willa probably knew that she wanted to write a book about it, but she did not talk much about it that summer at Grand Manan. She rarely discussed in advance anything she intended to write. According to Edith Lewis she occasionally outlined beforehand her plan for a novel but always left out "the secret treasure at its heart, the thing that gave it its reason for being."

Upon her return to New York that autumn, she began to write *Shadows on the Rock*. It was to be another book about pioneers, French pioneers this time, who founded a settlement on the Rock of Quebec in the seventeenth century. The similarity between their problems and those of the Nebraska pioneers was the thing that caught Willa Cather's emotions and imagination and made her want to write about them. It was not the settlement's very first years that she chose to write about. By 1697–98 the town of Quebec had grown to a population of close to two thousand—about the size of Red Cloud in Willa Cather's childhood. The problems of the first settlers remained, however, and her story, like her Nebraska stories, was about how people responded to new circumstances in a new society.

She was only a short way into the book when she realized she needed to return to Quebec for more material. This time she went alone. She interviewed historians and did so much reading that when she returned to New York two weeks later, she was suffering from eyestrain.

In December, only a year after her father's first heart attack, she received word from her brother Douglass in

California that her mother had suffered a paralytic stroke. Willa went there at once and found that her mother's mind was clear but that she was unable to speak. Willa rented a cottage on the grounds of the sanatorium in Pasadena where her mother was being cared for and remained there for many weeks.

Her distress over her mother's illness was so great that she could not continue with her work on *Shadows on the Rock*. During the months following her father's illness and death, her mind had turned back to Nebraska and she had written a story about a Bohemian farmer, which she called "Neighbor Rosicky." Now again her mind went back to those early years in Nebraska and she started two stories, "Two Friends" and "Old Mrs. Harris." The first was about two friends of her parents' whom she had known during her childhood in Red Cloud. "Old Mrs. Harris" was a portrait of her Grandmother Boak and of life in the Cather household in Red Cloud when Willa Cather and her brothers and sisters were growing up. Even these short works were too much for her in her distraught frame of mind, and they were not completed until 1931. They were published in 1932, along with "Neighbor Rosicky," in a volume called *Obscure Destinies*.

Although she could not write, she could read and did so, steeping herself in the history of Quebec and the French civilization there.

It was a year before she felt like writing again. In the winter of 1929–30 she made another visit to Quebec and when she returned to New York, she went back to work on the book. That spring she again visited her mother, whose condition had not improved. In May she sailed for France. She spent two months in Paris doing research for her book and visiting Isabelle Hambourg, who had become seriously ill.

When she returned to the United States in September

she chose the St. Lawrence route in order to catch another glimpse of Quebec. She found she could not pass it by and even though her trunks had gone on ahead of her, she decided to stay, buying what clothes she needed. During her visit to her mother that spring and her stay in France she had done no writing. Now the sight of Quebec, its strong French character still very much alive on this separate continent, brought Willa Cather very close to her story again. By the time she left for Jaffrey, she was impatient to begin writing.

The last part of *Shadows on the Rock* came easily and quickly. She finished it at the Grosvenor Hotel on December 27. It was published the following year, 1931, the same year that her mother died. Willa went to Red Cloud for the funeral. It was to be her last visit there. With her parents dead, with the family home broken forever, she could never bring herself to return to Nebraska.

sixteen

With the break-up of the family home in Red Cloud and the loss of the apartment in Bank Street, where she had spent her most productive writing years, Willa Cather's life was torn up by the roots. So long as her parents were alive and living in their Red Cloud home, she had felt that her life had a solid foundation even though the world around her was changing swiftly and taking directions she could not fit herself into. Now all that was changed. She felt herself adrift. There were Jaffrey and Grand Manan, but they were not permanent homes and were not meant to be. The Grosvenor Hotel, cramped and unattractive, was no longer tolerable.

In the fall of 1932 Willa and Edith Lewis took an

apartment on Park Avenue. She had never cared for Park Avenue—indeed she had never cared for any luxury—but she had allowed herself to be persuaded that this was where a writer of her stature should live. Ten year earlier no one could have persuaded her of any such thing, but the death of her parents, the long strain of her mother's illness, had cost Willa a great deal of her strength. She had begun to keep a small diary and all too often the words "Very tired" or "Deadly tired" appeared in it now.

She began to withdraw from the world. Visitors, even friends, found it more and more difficult to see her. She appeared to be isolating herself from people. Her response to them had always been intense and she could no longer spare the energy for these encounters.

She did keep alive her old friendships, particularly those with people back in Nebraska. She derived great pleasure from any opportunity to express her love for them. She felt some guilt at living in a luxurious New York apartment when her friends in Nebraska were suffering through the Great Depression and the worst drought the prairie states had ever known. She continued to send gifts to Anna Pavelka and to Mrs. Lambrecht, whose children had been her first playmates on the prairie and who had remained a good friend of the Cathers' after they moved into Red Cloud. Willa Cather had often sent Mrs. Lambrecht handmade woolen sweaters and scarves from abroad. Now she sent money to Red Cloud merchants with instructions to send Mrs. Lambrecht the special brand of coffee she liked, dried fruits, and other delicacies that Willa knew the Lambrechts would not be able to afford in those hard times.

She forgot none of her old friends and when any of them suffered a crop failure, she managed to find out about it and sent a check disguised as a valentine or as a birthday or Christmas gift.

She did form one new passionate relationship and afterward remarked that she would rather have had almost any other chapter of her life left out than this one which brought her so much happiness: her friendship with the Menuhins. Through Jan Hambourg she met this famous musical family in Paris during the summer of 1930. They were drawn to one another immediately. After Willa's return to the United States, Marutha Menuhin and her two daughters—Yalta, who was about seven, and Hephzibah, who was a year or two older—visited her, and the friendship developed rapidly. In the spring of 1931, while Willa was visiting her mother at the sanatorium in California, Yehudi Menuhin, then fifteen, paid her a visit. He and his father, Moshe, were giving a series of concerts across the country.

The Menuhin children were the most talented Willa had ever known. Yehudi's talent amounted to genius. He had given his first violin concert at Carnegie Hall when he was twelve. The children were also extremely lovable and unspoiled. It seemed that Willa, always fond of children, had at last acquired a family suited exactly to her taste. They were devoted to literature and art. Everything else was of secondary importance.

The three children had had a very strict upbringing in order to prevent their being spoiled by an adoring and curious public. They spent most of each day at their lessons and practicing and took walks with their mother in Central Park, sometimes as early as six in the morning in order to enjoy some privacy.

In writing of Willa's friendship with the Menuhins, Edith Lewis said: "I remember the Menuhin family's winter visits to New York in the years that followed as a sort of continuous festival, full of concerts and gay parties, orange trees and baskets of flowers for Willa Cather, arriving in the midst of snowstorms, birthday luncheons with Russian caviar and champagne, excursions to the opera where she took Yalta and Hephzibah to hear *Parsifal* for the first time, long walks around the reservoir in Central Park when the three children all wanted to walk beside her and had to take turn about. They discussed very abstract subjects together—art, religion, philosophy, life. If Willa Cather had been writing *War and Peace*, I'm sure she would have abandoned it to take these walks.

"She had a feeling that Hephzibah and Yalta, traveling in so many countries and learning something of the languages of each, were never going to get a thorough sense of the English language and this worried her. She asked Marutha Menuhin if she might organize a Shakespeare Club with no one allowed to be present except herself and the little girls. Yehudi then asked if he might come too. They began with *Richard II* and went on to *Macbeth* and *Henry IV*. Willa hunted through the bookstores of New York to get each of the children a copy of these plays in the original Temple edition, the only one she herself cared to read. It was then rapidly going out of print. She was greatly touched when many years afterwards Yehudi told her he had found and bought a complete secondhand set of the Temple Shakespeare in a shop in New Orleans."

During those unsettled, unhappy years she had lived at the Grosvenor Hotel, Willa had had little time for music. Once settled in her Park Avenue apartment, however, and with music brought back into her life by her friendship with the Menuhins, she could never hear enough of it. It once more became a source of happiness and comfort. When she was weary or depressed or under a strain, she would say, "I must have music." Her one concession to the machine age was her phonograph, given to her by Alfred Knopf and his wife. She bought records of

Beethoven and her other favorite composers, and Yehudi Menuhin sent her from England all the records he had made with his sister Hephzibah.

Her next book, *Lucy Gayheart*, grew out of this renewed musical world she wove around herself. It also grew out of a desire to live again in imagination some of those early years in Nebraska. The book went very slowly at first. Even though she felt the urge to write, her mind and body were heavy from the strain of the last few years. The result in the first chapters of the novel was a sluggishness that no amount of revision could lighten.

She began the book in New York in the spring of 1933. Moving to Grand Manan for the summer, she still had difficulty in bringing the story to life. It was only in Jaffrey, during the autumn months in the cool mountain air, that she began to feel herself again. From that time on the writing went smoothly and the first draft of the manuscript was completed quickly.

It was just as she was beginning revisions of this first draft that calamity struck. She developed an inflammation of the sheath surrounding the tendon in her right wrist. Her doctor devised a steel and leather brace that immobilized her thumb but permitted some small movement of the fingers. She could do little more than sign her name. Her book had to be set aside. Typing was impossible too, and she felt that she could not dictate a piece of creative writing to a secretary. Such words must flow from her hands.

Eventually the condition cleared enough that she could go back to working on her book, but she was never again completely free from this disability. It returned at intervals, most often to her right hand, but sometimes to her left. It made even the simplest, everyday tasks like bathing and opening letters difficult, but she refused to give over these tasks to others. Once when a friend offered to help, Willa told how even as a child, when her parents would try to assist her in something, she would cry, "Self alone! Self alone!"

By spring of 1934 her hand had recovered enough that she was able to finish the novel. Like Thea Kronborg in *The Song of the Lark*, Lucy Gayheart grows up in a small Nebraska town and leaves it to pursue a musical career in Chicago. Unlike Thea, however, Lucy does not have a great musical talent. Her gifts are an extraordinary fineness of nature and a passionate response to life and people. Thea's is a career story; Lucy's, a love story.

Lucy's story had lain in Willa Cather's mind for nearly thirty-seven years, ever since the night in 1896 when she had driven from Red Cloud to Blue Hill, a small town nearby, to attend a dance. There she met a young girl named Gayhardt who had come to Blue Hill to teach school. The two of them spent the evening discussing the classics and French literature. Willa felt that the delicate, sensitive girl was sadly out of her element in that rough prairie village.

Lucy Gayheart was published in 1935. Willa Cather did no writing that year. Isabelle Hambourg was still seriously ill and Willa Cather spent many months looking after her while she was in the United States and later in Paris. When Willa Cather took leave of her in Paris, it was a final parting. Isabelle died three years later.

Knowing her friend would never recover from her illness was another sorrow added to those she had already suffered, and another drain on her energy. She managed to bring out a book of essays, *Not Under Forty*, in 1936, and in 1937 wrote a long story called "The Old Beauty." She missed the companionship, the sense of purpose, a novel gives to a writer and in the fall of 1937 she began *Sapphira and the Slave Girl*. For the first time in her career she was turning to her Virginia background for material.

She began the book with much of her old power and

enthusiasm. By spring she felt that she must return to Virginia and visit the place where she had spent the first nine years of her life.

She found things very much changed. Willowshade, her old home, was now owned by a man who had always borne a grudge against it. He had cut down the willow trees that had given the place its name and chopped down the box hedges that Willa had loved as a child. The house was so run-down, so forlorn, that she did not go into it but stood and looked at it from a distance. None of this seemed to matter to her, however. She seemed able to look through outward appearances and see everything as it had been, even things she could not quite remember. The house at Mill Farm in which her grandparents had lived was still there, but the slave cabins had disappeared. The Boak place—her birthplace—was still shaded by maples and remained much as she remembered it.

Sapphira and the Slave Girl was not finished until 1940. During the writing blow after blow had been dealt to Willa. Her brother Douglass died suddenly, Isabelle also died, and World War II began. Even Jaffrey, her favorite writing spot, had been ripped apart by a hurricane.

Yet she kept at her book with a dogged determination, describing life as it had been in Virginia, not in her own childhood but during the period when her two grandmothers had been children. It is the story of slavery and the evil effects it has on both black and white people. But it is also the story of a slow-paced, graceful way of life that is gone forever. Willa Cather was often criticized for always writing of the past, for never dealing with the world in which she lived. It was a foolish criticism. Great writers do not choose their material; it grows unbidden within them from whatever the writer has experienced deeply and passionately.

In the case of Willa Cather, it was that first violent

uprooting from her home in Virginia that caused her eyes and heart ever after to turn backward. She was as much a pioneer as those Bohemians, Swedes, Germans, and Frenchmen she found on the prairie. All of them had left ordered and regulated lives to come to a raw, wild land. She, as well as they, longed for the comfort of familiar things left behind. To her the past was always something solid and fine, the present disorganized and even distasteful. She took the past and changed it into art.

During the seven years that were left to her after the completion of *Sapphira and the Slave Girl,* Willa's health grew more and more fragile. She worked on only two stories, one a sketch, the other a rough draft.

On April 24, 1947, she remained in bed and had lunch brought to her there. Except for her fatigue, she appeared normal and chatted alertly with Edith Lewis. She awoke from a nap later in the afternoon complaining of a severe head pain. Death came a few hours later. She was buried, as she had asked to be, in Jaffrey, New Hampshire.

It may seem strange that she did not want to be buried in Red Cloud with her parents, but the prairie, despite its hold over her, did not command her full love. It had frightened her when she first saw it and some of that fear remained with her the rest of her life. It was simply too vast. For Willa Cather it always held a menacing quality, almost as if it were crouching there, alive and monstrous, ready to spring. She once told Elizabeth Shepley Sergeant that although she became wildly homesick for the prairie and would rush back to see her family and the wheat harvest, she soon fled back East for fear that she might die in a cornfield. When Miss Sergeant expressed surprise at such a strange fear, Willa Cather told her that since she had not seen those miles of fields, she could not understand.

"There is no place to hide in Nebraska," she said. "You can't hide under a windmill."

Unlike the prairie, New England had been conquered and tamed by man, and in the process it had acquired a long and rich past. Jaffrey, Willa Cather's adopted home, had been incorporated as a village in 1773. Its enormous church, known as "The Old Meetinghouse," had been raised on the day of the Battle of Bunker Hill. All its wildness had long since been subdued. The roughness was gone, graciousness and charm had taken its place. One could feel safe there. Willa Cather knew that in Jaffrey she could lie in peace.

Carved into the pure white stone marking Willa Cather's grave is a quotation from *My Ántonia:*

". . . . . . . That is happiness; to be dissolved into something complete and great."

bibliography

Bennett, Mildred R. *The World of Willa Cather* (New edition with notes and index). Lincoln, Nebraska: University of Nebraska Press, 1961.

Brown, E. K. *Willa Cather: A Critical Biography*, completed by Leon Edel. New York: Alfred A. Knopf, 1953.

Lewis, Edith. *Willa Cather Living*. New York: Alfred A. Knopf, 1953.

Sergeant, Elizabeth Shepley. *Willa Cather: A Memoir*. Lincoln, Nebraska: University of Nebraska Press, 1960.

Slote, Bernice. *The Kingdom of Art: Willa Cather's First Principles and Critical Statements 1893–1896*. Lincoln, Nebraska: University of Nebraska Press. 1966.

index

about the author

Barbara Bonham was born September 27, 1926, in Franklin, Nebraska. She received her primary and secondary education in the Franklin public schools and later attended the University of Nebraska. Following that she worked for four years as an office nurse for a doctor in Franklin. It was during that period that she enrolled in a correspondence course in writing. Three years later she sold her first story. For the next ten years she continued to write, selling more than seventy-five stories.

In 1962 she began writing historical fiction and non-fiction for children. *Challenge of the Prairie*, published in 1965, and *Crisis at Fort Laramie*, published in 1967, were the result of this interest.

Her great-grandparents were pioneers who traveled in a covered wagon and homesteaded on the prairie about thirty miles northwest of Willa Cather's Red Cloud in 1872. Barbara Bonham was born and reared a few miles from the homestead and as a result the prairie and its history are part of her blood and bone. Even though she belongs to a different generation than Willa Cather, she can still see many things in it that Miss Cather saw.

Mrs. Bonham and her husband live on a farm near Naponee, Nebraska.